CLINICS CLOUD IN THE

How smart business owners in private practice take the pain out of marketing, increase profitability and attract more ideal clients online.

Yalcin Yilmaz

Clinics in the Cloud – How smart business owners in private practice take the pain out of marketing, increase profitability and attract more ideal clients online.

Copyright ©2014 Yalcin Yilmaz
V1.2 published 2014, Catapult Interactive, Australia

Paperback ISBN: 978-0-9925518-0-3
Editor: Todd Barselow
Illustrations: Xhenxhen
Cover design: Arturo Alvarez Rios
Interior design: Yalcin Yilmaz
Subjects: Small business, Marketing, Online marketing, Healthcare marketing, Business coaching

Disclaimer: While the author has used their best efforts in preparing this book, no representations or warranties are made with respect to the accuracy or completeness of the contents of this book. The advice and strategies contained herein may not be suitable for your situation. You should consult with a professional where appropriate.

I would like to thank all my clients who have trusted me to be a part of their business. Seeing the right ideas and strategies implemented at the right time to transform businesses has been quite an experience!

Dedicated to Yasemin and Elif.

Table of contents

Introduction	**15**
The only constant is change	17
Embracing change	19
What is the "Cloud" and how can it help you?	22
Who this book is for	23
How to use this book	25
The untold joys of business life in private practice	**27**
Why did you take the plunge?	30
How do you feel about it?	30
Things they never taught you at university!	31
Working "ON" the business	32
Establishing a business mindset	34
You're a local business	36
Your hidden competition	38
Work-life balance	39
Getting empowered	39
Seeking advice	40
Set attainable goals, one at a time	41
Asking for help	42
Getting things done	42
The 3 Ps of online strategy for private practice	**45**
1) Presence: Your online business platform	48
2) Publish: Content creation	49
3) Profile: Getting the word out	50

Presence: Your online business platform   **53**

Your website: The mother ship   55
 Lead generation   58
 Lead conversion   59

Getting online   60
 Your new practice website   64
 Do you already have a website?   67
 Multiple websites for multiple locations   70

Your domain name   71
 Types of domain names   71
 Choosing a good domain name   72
 Registering a domain name   74

Hosting   76

Email accounts   76
 Security and spam   77

Looking good   77
 Who are you designing for?   78
 Important design factors   79
 A winning formula   79

Must-have pages   81
 Homepage   82
 Persistent information   83
 About your practice   84
 Educational material   85
 Marketing and promotion   86
 Images and video   87

Turning visitors into sales   87
 Clear the path   88
 Get attention   89
 Make them comfortable   89
 Call-to-action (CTA)   90
 Landing pages   91

Start a relationship   92
Should you sell stuff on your website?   93

What to avoid on your website   94

Building your website   95
Choosing a web developer   95
Evolution and growth   96
WordPress and other CMS   97
Updates and security   100
Disaster planning and recovery   100
Ongoing support   100

What will all this cost?   101

Setting your expectations   102
What not to expect   103

Publish: Content creation   **105**

Importance of content   107
Types of content   109
What makes good content?   110
Getting others to write   114
Integrating sales   115

Content distribution   116
Be prolific   116
Be found online   118

Your practice blog   119
Why should you blog?   120
How to start a blog   122
What do you say?   123
Blogging tips   125

Online video   130
Why do video?   132
Video for local private practice   134
Types of video to produce   135

Planning ahead 137
Things you'll need 139
Action! 147
Post-production 149
Exporting and uploading 153
Maximum value 155
Video tips 157
Getting professionals 158
Other content offerings 159
EBooks 159
Information sheets 160
Screencasts, webinars and podcasts 160
Your publishing rhythm 161

Profile: Getting the word out **163**
Outbound vs. inbound marketing 166
Importance of regular contact 171
Search Engines 172
How search engines work 174
The search results page 175
Living to 100 years old 176
Search Engine Optimisation (SEO) basics 180
Local SEO 188
Getting help 191
Email marketing 193
What you need 194
Your email list 195
Do you have permission? 196
What to send 200
Composing your marketing emails 204
Email design 207
Keeping your list clean 208

Micro-targeted communication 210
Mobile marketing 211
The "mobile user" 213
Your mobile-optimised website 214
What about SMS? 216
Location-Based Marketing 218
QR codes 219
Mobile apps 221
Pay-Per-Click: Paid advertising 222
Advantages of PPC 222
Disadvantages of PPC 223
How PPC works 225
Google AdWords 226
Google AdWords Express 230
Facebook advertising 231
Social Media 232
Part of the marketing puzzle 233
Importance of social proof 235
It's a marathon, not a sprint 236
Throw a party 237
Facebook 238
Facebook for business 240
Your Facebook Page 241
Posting to your Facebook Page 244
Events, Offers, Contests and Groups 248
Check ins 251
Google+ 252
Google+ for business 254
SEO and other benefits of Google+ 257
Your Google+ Page 259
Posting to your Google+ Page 264
Communities, Hangouts & Events 267
Check ins 268

Reviews 268

YouTube 270
YouTube for business 271
Your YouTube Channel 271
Uploading videos to your channel 275
Video SEO 277
Getting mileage from your videos 279

Other social channels 281
LinkedIn 281
Twitter 281
Pinterest 282
Instagram 283
Foursquare 284

"Getting" social media 284
Building social momentum 287
Your posting rhythm 287
Getting your first followers 289
Shares, likes, +1s, thumb ups & comments 289
Engaging with your followers 291
Privacy and security 293

Citations, reviews and reputation 293
NAP: Name, address and phone 293
Directories and review sites 294
Reputation management 295

Crossing your channels 296

Testing and measuring 299
Key indicators 301
Tools of the trade 302
Google Analytics 303
Google Webmaster Tools 304
Social media measurement 304

Measuring promotions   305
    Landing pages   305
    A-B testing   306
    Personalised URLs   307
    Making sense of data   308

Ethics and legal   **311**
    Use of copyrighted material   313

About the author   **315**
    About PracticePulse   316

Book website

In the digital age things are never at a standstill. Links expire, new ideas are born, and the Internet keeps evolving. That's why I developed a destination website for this book. Visit **clinicsinthecloud.com** for additional tools, updates or corrections, new resources and more. You can also submit questions and share your own resource tips.

Of course, you're welcome to visit our business website **practicepulse.com** to see how we help businesses like yours.

Conventions

Australian terminology and conventions are used throughout the book. You might refer to your business as a "practice" rather than a "clinic". You may refer to yourself as a "physical therapist" instead of a "physiotherapist". Maybe you went to college instead of university. You may "inquire" rather than "enquire". Depending on your business, you may refer to your customers as "patients" instead of "clients". It is safe to ignore differences like these. You know what I mean.

Introduction

Change is constant. It's also what many fear most. Change is necessary if deep inside you feel your business has the potential to be more. If your business isn't giving you the payoff you want, dream about and deserve, then embracing change can change that. Your business doesn't improve by chance, it improves through change. But how can you choose change that's right for you and your business?

This book aims to introduce you to all the "digital stuff" you've heard about but perhaps were too shy to ask about or thought was too hard to learn. It's designed to serve as a springboard to launch you toward making life easier and your practice more successful. Some of the ideas and concepts will be simple for you and others will seem baffling in the beginning. Go with what's easiest or what makes the most sense to you first before you introduce more complexity into the process.

The only constant is change

Technology puts tremendous leverage at your fingertips. Today, farmers in India have access to more technology in the palms of their hands than NASA had for its Apollo 11 mission to land the first man on the moon. A teenager sitting in her bedroom has more tools for building a global enterprise than Coca-Cola did when it started international expansion. A start-up entrepreneur can quickly and easily test and validate markets and complex client demographics without spending a single dollar on marketing or even a trial service or prototype.

Not long ago even email was cutting edge. I remember sending my first email back in 1992, and also my first brick of a mobile phone in 1996. Twenty years ago if I asked you how many feet were in a mile (and you didn't know) you could go to a library and look it up in a book. Ten years ago, you could look it up on your computer. Today, you can literally ask your phone.

I belong to Generation X: those souls responsible for kick-starting the rate of change increase. However, it's Generation Y (having come of age between 1998-2006), who have contributed the most to the exponential growth in today's rate of change.

Generation Y is impatient, inquisitive and quick to grasp new things. They're partly lazy, hence they're always looking for easier ways to accomplish stuff faster while using fewer resources. They also notice problems quicker and tend to question the status quo. They adapt aggressively and embrace change faster than us older people do.

Various technology and paradigms have become woven into the very fabric of our society. Tweeting, texting, friending, following, Googling, tagging, trending, uploading, sharing and checking-in have become familiar verbs (alas, to the dismay of grammarians).

Generation Z will take all that even further. If you've ever been on a bus or train full of students from the local school behaving like a wild herd, you probably questioned the future of your country. However, they're so fine-tuned to change and so ready to adapt that we'll likely be questioning our own place in **their** world by the time they're adults.

> "It is not the strongest of the species that survive, nor the most intelligent, but the one that proves itself most responsive to change."
> ~ Leon Megginson (referencing C. Darwin's On the Origin of Species.)

Recently, I was sitting on a plane with my family awaiting take-off from Melbourne Airport. After sitting there for 2 minutes, my 6 year-old sighed impatiently and said, "Oh man, what is the hold up!" to which my 3 year-old casually remarked, "It's just loading..." – like her iPad apps that take a little time to "load" before she could play with them.

For a bit of fun, search for "baby thinks magazine is iPad" over at YouTube and watch how traditional media is already so foreign for this little guy.

Embracing change

All these online tools, services and applications have brought new ways of doing things, new arenas for marketing and meaningful interaction and better ways for measuring their effectiveness. Marketers and businesses of 20 years ago couldn't possibly dream of what is now common practice.

Knowledge is no longer power – it can be attained so easily via a computer or smartphone. It doesn't really matter if I know the answer to a given question. What matters is that information can be fed reliably and directly to me from an external source. There is no longer an advantage to remembering stuff. After asking the right questions, you just need to apply logic, reasoning and decision making to reach your outcomes.

Even though it may look chaotic, change is deliberate and organic. It's driven by needs. For example, did you know that neither Facebook nor Twitter were initially intended for business use? And mobile phones have become a massive target of localised information delivery – much more than their original intent – simply making phone calls.

Along with ubiquity, there has also been a spike in democracy. Users aren't afraid to voice their opinion. They know they have options and will freely give their opinions. Large corporations can no longer hide behind call centres for customer support or rely on old-school marketing for growth. Now a small business can have the professional presence and branding of big corporations thanks to advancements in technology. It doesn't matter whether you're a one-person operator or a company of 500 employees – you can easily and affordably stand up and be counted. You can also host, cater to and participate in meaningful interactions with customers online, cost effectively. You no longer need to spend thousands of dollars on a full-page Yellow Pages ad in order to stand out. All you need are some (affordable) tools and an Internet connection.

Also, customers are increasingly demanding businesses be online and up-to-date before even engaging with them. Amazon now sells more eBooks than physical books. Whatever happened to Borders and other bricks-and-mortar bookshops?

"We shape our tools, and our tools shape us."
~ John Culkin

Technology is real and those that fail to embrace it are being left behind. Reporting on Australia's National Digital Economy Strategy, iTwire.com wrote: "The comprehensive transition of Australia's economy and society to a digital economy is appropriately a market-led phenomenon. Maximising the benefit of the digital economy requires action by all levels of government, industry and the community as a whole."

Governments, corporations, consumers and other local businesses are leveraging technology like never before. **The question is, what about YOUR business?**

If you're pre-Gen Y and feel a little left-behind – you're not alone! Remember this fact: as a health professional, you make people feel better, make them healthier and help them lead a fuller existence. You went to university and got a degree. You're obviously smart! Private practice owners less experienced than you are using all these new tools to run successful practices. You're doing your community a disservice by not being visible!

You just need to know your options, learn enough to be able to evaluate and choose where you want to spend your energy and use the available tools in their simplest form.

Of course you can still have a successful business without embracing smart technology – just like it's possible to have a large patient base by virtue of great location or connections. But it won't be sustainable. Perhaps that's why you've picked up this book – you're looking for smarter ways to grow your business.

Remember, everything is hard before it's easy; you learned to dress yourself as a kid, ride a bike and drive a car. With a little work, you can make big things happen.

What is the "Cloud" and how can it help you?

The "cloud" refers to using the Internet to access various tools, services and data storage. It's called such because it's pretty much available anywhere and you don't really need to know how it works – all you need to know is that you can get done what you need to get done affordably by using it.

For example, when you access your Gmail account, you're using the cloud as Gmail is not stored or installed on your computer. You can access your emails from anywhere with an Internet connection and a browser. Things like Facebook and other social media are also "in the cloud". Becoming a part of the cloud essentially means offering benefits to your clients.

Since software and data storage is handled by some online entity, you don't need to worry about upgrades, security or accessibility. You only need to focus on using the tools to your advantage.

> "The future is already here. It just isn't evenly distributed."
> ~ William Gibson

The cloud concept makes it easier to run businesses. It's fast, revolutionary and accountable, all without breaking the bank.

Who this book is for

This book is designed for private practice owners (e.g. physiotherapists, podiatrists, chiropractors, osteopaths dentists, acupuncturists, massage therapists, psychologists etc.) who want more out of their business.

Here you'll discover how successful practice owners:

- Attract more ideal clients and more referrals.
- Stand out as an authority / leader in their field.
- Improve productivity.
- Create and implement online marketing strategy on a shoestring budget.
- Evaluate and exploit new and emerging trends.

You will learn:

- The essential elements of a website that sells.
- The importance of content and communication.
- What it takes to rank well in Google.
- How to get new clients from social media.
- To create and promote videos for massive online exposure.
- Email marketing to increase your client base.
- And much more.

This book was designed to help you take charge and gain necessary knowledge so you can understand how to use this technical stuff to your advantage. It'll help you become empowered, informed and confident discussing your strategy and requirements with qualified consultants and suppliers. It'll help you recognise the impact of your online strategy on your practice and evaluate new and emerging ideas.

> You don't need to become a guru to use the tools.

The goal here is not to turn you into an Internet guru. This book is designed to show you how you can get the maximum return for limited time and money invested while your practice gives you the lifestyle you want and dream about.

All you need are some of the proven tools discussed here. When you grasp the concepts behind them, it will be a light bulb moment and you'll simply get it.

The best thing about this? You can choose how 'hands on' you want to be. If you're a tinkerer like me, you want to get your hands dirty and learn how to do things for yourself.

Another option is to use consultants who specialise in websites and online presence for private practice. With the right professionals, this option will actually save you time and money.

Many of our clients at PracticePulse appreciate that we provide these services cost effectively.

> I founded PracticePulse in 2008 with a vision to help businesses in private practice build healthier communities. Having been asked the same questions daily and seeing business owners driving with their handbrakes up prompted me to write this book.

Whatever you decide, I hope that this book will educate and inspire you with what's possible. Don't just embrace what you read or hear with blind enthusiasm – evaluate it. Try it out and see if it's for you.

How to use this book

Having started this chapter discussing change, it's worth noting that everything referred to in this book could well have changed by the time you read it. So take it as a guide on your path to enlightenment and empowerment. The concepts will hold true.

There is no one size fits all solution. Each practice is different. Every business owner is unique. So, pick what makes sense to you and run with what works for you. That said, feel free to jump ahead to the parts of this book that interest you.

I hope you're excited! Here you'll learn how to go from the business you have today to a business that gives you more options and a better work-life balance tomorrow.

The untold joys of business life in private practice

Congratulations, you have a business! While many practice owners love what they do, they often struggle with juggling too many balls to keep the doors open. Many feel that they aren't getting anywhere. This isn't why you went to university. But, how do you move forward from here?

The only exercise I do to get my heart rate up is to stress out at work

If you're like most business owners in private practice then the desire to treat people and alleviate their pains gives you untold joy and satisfaction. That's why you're in business! But then there are things like marketing, advertising, client promotions, administration work, staff issues and 'business fires' that make your life miserable.

It would be nice if you could delegate all those necessary evils to a capable staff member. That would certainly make your life easier. But that's a luxury most understaffed and sometimes underpaid practice owners cannot afford ... so guess who picks up the tab?

Oops...there's another late night.

Honey, why are you late for dinner ... again!

Where are the kids? They're in bed, fast asleep.

One day, you'll have the life you thought you would by now...

Okay, so you have a problem. Your business isn't really the sleek machine that gives you a happy lifestyle – it's a demanding and often stressful job.

Fortunately, there's life at the end of the tunnel!

One business expert says that most practices don't work – the people who own them do. Well, I say it's time to reclaim your life!

Over the next pages you'll learn some simple online business tools – stuff you know or heard about but never got around to trying out for one reason or another – that will help to get your life back and make your business more successful. But first you need to get clear about why...

Why did you take the plunge?

Clarity provides focus. I find the fastest way of getting onto the right track again is to revisit your passions and life goals.

Why did you get into business?

- Because being your own boss gives you more freedom and control (at least that's what you thought!)
- To have more flexible working hours.
- You can provide excellent client care on your terms.
- To raise your financial ceiling.

Go on; take a moment to ruminate on those reasons. Think about where you are today in your business and where you want to be. Don't worry about the gap right now, even if it scares you a bit.

How do you feel about it?

Here's what I often hear from private practice clients and business consultants:

- Not enough business or cash flow.
- Not enough autonomy, time, resources or control.
- Feeling overwhelmed with too many things to take care of.
- Stuck with a model that's not working.
- Feeling devalued as a professional.
- Cutting too many corners to make ends meet.
- Running out of time, money and patience.

It's exhausting to build a financially, professionally and personally rewarding business and still have time for family and friends.

It's not all doom and gloom as many people in private practice are living a happy business life.

- Their business is predictable, profitable and fun.
- They feel good about the future, with a sense of stability.
- They enjoy great relationships with patients.
- Their business success makes them feel proud.

Which boxes have you ticked? Chances are you need to make some changes in your business. Perhaps instead of being a dream vehicle, your business resembles a vehicle with flat tyres. Sure, you're moving but it can be such a struggle!

Sometimes it can be as easy as pumping up the flat tyres in your business. Many of my clients are surprised to learn how quickly and easily they can get on the right track the moment they put technology to good use in their business.

Things they never taught you at university!

Education is greatly overpriced in our culture.

There is a general belief that if you master a discipline, do the hard yards and study hard then you can look forward to a bright future.

The reality is that school doesn't prepare you for the real world. It definitely won't give you the 'street smarts' you need to be a success in business. You have a great gift – but struggle trying to reach people with it.

Working "ON" the business

Here's your big business dilemma.

To be successful in business, YOU need to work ON your business. Providing outstanding patient care (working IN the business) should be your secondary focus. Why? Because to treat patients you first need to find enough patients, for without them your business won't stay afloat.

Business isn't always common sense. What helps is to identify the key elements in your business that you need to focus on. Every business requires:

- **Sales & marketing** – generating leads and converting to paying clients.
- **Delivery** – delivering the quality service clients want to pay for... i.e. what they taught you at university.
- **Facilities, staffing & administration** – what happens in the background to keep your business running smoothly.

Key elements of your business:

Sales & Marketing

Service
Delivery

Facilities,
Staffing
& Admin

Stretching all 3 areas will yield biggest results.

Your facilities (location, rooms etc.) may be pretty much fixed, or can be very expensive to implement significant changes to. We will assume that your delivery (i.e. patient results, your professional and technical skills) is already on par. The remaining part of the puzzle where there is unlimited opportunity is in sales and marketing.

Ignoring sales and marketing could mean closure of your business altogether, even if you're a top-grade practitioner.

If you're feeling a little intimated, remember:

- It's not as hard as you think – all you need is guidance.
- It's not as expensive or time consuming as you think.
- It's an ongoing process – not a one-off event.
- Practical help *is* available (for do-it-yourself types and delegators).
- Marketing and sales are not evil – they are necessary activities for the success of your business.

The Internet gives you access to new markets or niches. The KEY is to get to those markets first ... before your competitors do.

This book will show you how.

Establishing a business mindset

You've probably heard of the KISS formula (Keep It Simple Stupid). The reason why many busy practice owners continue to struggle is because they overcomplicate their business existence.

What I've learned by studying some of the greatest minds in business marketing is that there are only 3 ways to grow a business:

- You need to get more clients (marketing)
- Sell more to those clients or charge more (education)
- Get those clients to buy your services more often (communication and automation)

Improvement	None	10%	20%
Clients per month	500	550	600
Average fee	$50	$55	$60
Revenue	$25,000	$30,250	$36,000
Change in revenue	0%	21%	44%

Just improving the number of clients you see each month by 10% and raising your fees by 10% gives you not 20% but 21% increase in revenue. Raising them by 20% increases your revenue by 44%. You can see how working on multiple aspects to your business can have a compounding effect.

Similarly, let's imagine that your website gets 1000 visitors per month, from which you get 5 enquiries (0.5% conversion).

If you simply:

1. Increase your traffic by 20% (e.g. better placement in Google, better links etc.)
2. Double your website's conversion to 1% (better information, easier to use, better design, clear prompts etc.)
3. Implement a regular monthly newsletter with 500 subscribers and 5% conversion.

You would get 1200 website visitors total; with the doubled 1% conversion, it would result in 12 enquiries. Plus 25 enquiries from your newsletters and you have a total of 28 appointments. This is 7.4 times the enquiries you were getting before.

> Small gains over a variety of areas equates to larger gains overall.

This isn't hard to achieve and it's easily sustainable month after month with little work. We haven't even touched on any other stuff you can do, such as mobile marketing and social media. That's where it could really take off.

You don't have to be a marketing genius when you start growing your business by small controlled increments in strategic areas. That's why here I will show you how to grow your business in ALL three areas. You'll learn how to improve your marketing, sales and automation processes to grow your business exponentially.

You may not feel comfortable marketing or want to work with fewer but better paying clients. This book is designed to help you choose the strategies you feel most comfortable with.

You're a local business

Being a "local business" is a major consideration when it comes to how you market, grow and run your business.

Your physical location (being in a heavy-traffic area) makes a big difference in the start-up phase of your business because people will notice you as they walk or drive past. This is low hanging fruit; but having a prime location won't necessarily book you solid. Especially if you have a handful of competitors in close proximity.

That's why having a strong online presence can make such a difference. People will search for and find you online – if you don't show up in the top Google searches or on your smartphone's map app, you virtually (pun intended) don't exist.

A professional online strategy can help you:

1. Get more clients without the angst.
2. Increase your fees and charge more by educating your patients and demonstrating your value.
3. Increase the average client visits and referrals through ongoing communication and education.

Your geographic location is also an important factor in your ongoing approach to online marketing. This is simply because unlike some other businesses, your clients will always need to come and see you in person to receive your services. This feature of your offering carries its own set of advantages and challenges online.

It also brings exciting opportunities, with the advent of mobile marketing and location-aware technology.

You need to earn trust to earn a living

Trust is invaluable. Being able to earn trust in your community can be the difference between paying for expensive business space and having a thriving business. Other physicians are happy to refer business your way and more clients do the same by spreading positive word of mouth. That won't happen by accident. People won't go out of their way to help you, but they will enthusiastically endorse and refer you to others the moment you develop a solid reputation.

Concepts in this book explore how to increase trust and raise your authority.

Referrals

Referrals are excellent for business. However, if you are receiving most of your income from referrals, then your marketing is not working. What would happen if one day your key referrer went out of business?

Referrals are great low-hanging fruit, and you would be wise to pursue them. However, they shouldn't be your sole (or primary) source of income.

Your hidden competition

Have you ever wondered why people are reluctant to spend $100 with you but will spend more than that on a night out or pay-TV subscription? What's wrong with people?

One reason for this is the lack of client awareness and education regarding the benefits you can provide, what you offer and what it could do for their lives.

Health professionals need to upgrade their profiles and be recognised for the results that they deliver. This can't be done by sitting on the sidelines, expecting business to come to you. You need to take a proactive stance in your profession. Don't allow bias, misinformation, self-diagnosis or recommendations from well-meaning friends dilute what you do as a profession.

You need to be able to explain what you do in plain English. The problem is that the average Joe doesn't get what you do, or worse, he has hidden bias or misconceptions about it. It surprises me how many practice owners don't take that seriously. This creates a lack of public awareness that results in further misunderstanding and hinders your ability to attract more clients, especially those who would greatly benefit from your services.

Even with awareness of what you do, the majority of the public tend to have a reactionary stance to their health. They may visit a chiropractor when they have a bad back, or a dentist when they chip a tooth. There is very little mind-space allocated for important services like these at other times, even with the tremendous benefits of proactive care.

That's another reason why ongoing education is so important. And having a professional website that educates your prospective clients 24/7 is one of the best ways to achieve this. They're going to be researching their problems online anyway – wouldn't you rather have them ON YOUR website?

Work-life balance

The reality is that business life isn't a walk in the park. Often, you need to juggle your personal and family responsibilities with those of running the business.

And since we all have a limited number of hours in the day, you need to consider what you want to do and what you want someone else to do for you.

> Never be too proud to seek help from other professionals. After all, your primary focus is to treat clients; outsourcing other stuff will give you more time.

Getting empowered

Ideas are very important, yet fragile. It's a tragedy when ideas die because you don't know how to bring them to life. When you have an idea about marketing and growing your practice, you should be able to test it out – it may turn out be the best thing you've done. You need to be able to then learn from that and continue growing it or try another idea.

A good starting point is simply becoming aware of your available options. As you open your eyes, you will begin to make connections and start seeing benefits of and synergies between your options. You can then start with low-hanging fruit and get your hands dirty. This could be something as simple as taking a look at your website's Content Management System and figuring out that when you save changes, your website's home page is updated.

When you get a good handle on what you are doing then you can try to be a little bit more ambitious. Once you are comfortable, you will be able to make informed choices and tweak your strategy accordingly.

The goal is to try new things, get some experience and feedback and grow from there. Getting empowered is what it's all about; finally catching up with everything that you felt left behind on. Being responsible and accountable for your business' success and direction and knowing that it didn't happen by chance would be a great feeling!

It need not be an uphill battle. Your website need not be a useless, aged piece of technology purchased long ago on a promise never delivered. You should be able to speak with someone who can execute your ideas, guide you or offer tools and support. You want to be able to implement easily and effectively, and see measurable results.

Seeking advice

Have you ever thought about turning your knowledge into a saleable asset or a viral marketing tool to help book yourself solid? What if you could jump on the social media bandwagon? Perhaps you're thinking, "What is social media anyway?"

Chances are there are so many tools that you have never considered using simply because you didn't know they existed. My goal here is not to give you every tool under the sun. I want to introduce you to the most common (lowest hanging fruit) strategies and tools that you can put to use the very next day!

Set attainable goals, one at a time

When you see all the wonderful tools and strategies that await you on the next pages you may get excited. Technology can be fascinating!

But don't forget, your goal is to simplify your life and make your business more successful – not become a technology geek or guru!

You want to leverage technology, not become enslaved by it. Along those lines, here are some tips to help you use technology wisely:

- Try things, one at a time.
- Get confident, do more things later.
- Some have prerequisite steps, so you need to be aware of what is needed along the way.
- Measure results. See what works – for you.
- Go a little bit deeper, gradually.
- Don't overwhelm yourself or your resources.

So, let me repeat this one more time. You should crawl before you walk and walk before you run – not the other way around! Getting 1 million views for your new clinic video should be exciting but perhaps generating 5 or 10 extra appointments per month from videos you shot and uploaded to YouTube is a good start.

Asking for help

There is nothing more refreshing and reassuring than having a knowledgeable expert by your side, helping you navigate the dark tunnels of new, often intimidating technology.

Seek the help of an experienced Internet strategy and web-development company who understands your needs and has been through it before with private practice businesses just like yours. The pace should be comfortable, yet proactive; you don't need to be overwhelmed. They should be patient, responsive, provide accountability and give you answers in plain English.

Even if you know exactly what to do on your own, with unlimited access to all the ideas and how-to videos and blogs online, you may simply not have the time or patience to get through everything.

Shameless plug: Take a look at **PracticePulse.com** – we work exclusively with businesses in private health practice. If you choose not to work with us then be sure not to accept any less from others.

Don't be afraid to ask for help – with the right help your business will grow faster and easier while you focus on what you do best – helping your clients.

Getting things done

Most private practice owners don't have the time or knowledge for marketing. Marketing is taboo to them. They consider it tedious, fruitless or a secret. Hence, they often simply default to "not doing stuff".

But sticking your head in the sand and hoping for better is not an option. Market fragmentation and increasing competition means that you need to have several "touches" with different groups of people to address their questions and establish your expertise.

Technology often introduces new levels of complexity, but also new opportunities. So, if you're a little intimidated by the social media and Internet stuff then you're not alone. Chances are that your competitors are just as perplexed!

"It is not enough to be industrious; so are the ants. What are you industrious about?"
~ Henry David Thoreau

Acting early and overtaking them will give you an advantage. That's why speed is so important. Otherwise you may become another victim of "paralysis-by-analysis"; it's what happens when you become aware of all your opportunities but don't have a practical implementation plan in place.

Someone once said "90% done and out the door is better than 100% never launched." Resolve to change things. Instead of striving for perfection, work towards being effective – there's a difference!

The 3 Ps of online strategy for private practice

The Internet has created a new breed of consumer. More educated and empowered, these consumers are looking for businesses that provide real value and relationships, with an online presence that satisfies them on many levels. As a practice owner, you need an integrated and holistic approach to your business online.

Harold was happy with his website performance

In the previous chapter, we covered the basics of a website, like domain names, email accounts, design and basic content. But this is only a beginning. This is where most businesses stop and wonder why their website is not bringing them clients. The website is a tool, and it is up to the practice owner to use it properly. Of course, some tools work better than others.

You need a strategy, consisting of:

1. Goal setting, client considerations, branding, building your platform.
2. Establishing authority and trust in your market.
3. Being found in search engines.
4. Local market focus.
5. Ensuring that people don't forget you.

Your online strategy is represented neatly as the 3 Ps.

The 3 Ps:

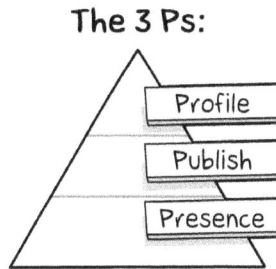

The key point is that the pieces build on top of each other and ultimately work together as a complete system. **Having the right tools, advice and support empowers you and helps you get things done and reach your goals faster.**

> 80% of online success comes from good strategy – knowing what to do and doing it.

The 3 Ps are explored in detail over the following 3 chapters.

1) Presence: Your online business platform

Your website is the major component of your online presence. However, there are many considerations to getting online.

Getting online requires you to be clear on your goals. Do you simply want more clients? Or do you want specific clients you're better qualified to serve than others in your field? Do you want more recognition among your peers? Do you want more referrals? Are you planning to sell your practice in the next few years?

Then you need to consider your clients' needs – what will they be looking for? What questions will they have? How will they find you online? Is your branding and presentation suitable?

It's important to think of your presence (your website) as an online business platform. It forms the basis of the 3 Ps. It needs to be adaptable and allow you to do the things you want to do now and also help you try new ideas in the future.

2) Publish: Content creation

Publishing is one of the best ways you can build credibility. Don't let that scare you – publishing isn't something reserved for the elite authors of the world. Think of it as "content creation".

The Internet has made publishers of the most unlikely people – even kids with mobile phone cameras or housewives posting to basic blogs. The mechanics aren't hard, really

Publishing can be in many forms; it's not limited to books and other printed material. You can create blog posts, online videos and eBooks as well as educational articles.

At first, these may appear to require significant time and effort. However, remember that they'll become a part of your intellectual property. They'll serve you in establishing yourself as an authority in your field, among clients, peers and referrers.

You already know your stuff – you went to university to get educated to do what you're doing. There are dozens of topics you can publish about.

It seems scary at first, picturing of yourself as someone who publishes stuff (after all, we're all used to consuming these things, not creating them). Just start with something simple, like a 300 word article (one page) covering a question that your clients ask all the time. If you're comfortable standing in front of a camera, it would take you less than half hour to discuss your topic and upload to YouTube. Maybe you're the blogging type, and can pump out small but regular posts.

In most cases, it's impressive enough that you've committed to publishing something, since most other people in your industry haven't. It doesn't have to be a unique topic – it just needs to be "yours". The key here is to publish stuff that people want or value. If you don't know what that is, sit down and have a think.

Now compare, in your mind, two versions of your website. One is an online brochure with 5 pages of "about us" and sales talk, and the other has dozens of pages of useful, original material, easy to understand videos or downloadable files and shareable posts. Which do you think will build more authority for you and your practice?

When done right, content creation builds trusting and loyal relationships with your target audiences by filling a knowledge void. This in turn drives you toward the ultimate goal of increasing sales or getting new referrals/clients.

Publishing and content creation has another significant benefit. It allows you be found via search engines. The topic of search engines is extensive and very important – so it's covered in detail later in this book. However, suffice it to say that the more material you publish online equates to more material that will be found and linked back to you.

3) Profile: Getting the word out

After having established your presence and started building your authority via publishing, you now have a good basis to capture and convert visitors to clients via your website.

People are bombarded with marketing messages and unwanted noise every day. It's getting harder to stand out and draw attention. This is especially true if there isn't enough public awareness of your profession and how you can help.

It is a bitter pill to swallow, but with all the competition for attention people will forget about you. You need to forge regular communication channels with your clients and prospects – without adding to the noise they already endure.

Getting into the habit of publishing great material is the first and biggest step. By providing answers and valuable information and insights or helping your audience solve some of their problems is by far the best way to cut through the noise, get and maintain attention. Everyone welcomes regular communication when it's useful and timely.

Regardless of what anyone says, email marketing is still one of the best ways to market to your audience. There's a whole section in this book about email marketing.

The boom of social media should not come as a surprise really – it enables people to communicate and keep up-to-date with things that are important to them. Sure, it's somewhat superficial and lazy, but it's so convenient for the introverts and extraverts alike. The fact that businesses have now followed social media trends to get amongst their consumers is no surprise (in hindsight) either.

Social media is perfect for content publishing, where sharing and word of mouth are built in. Crafting your profile in social circles is a fantastic way to reach more prospects and keep existing relationships strong.

One other thing: Remembering that your business is geo-centric in nature, building a local profile for your business is very important. Being found when people in your community need your services is vital for your business success.

Presence: Your online business platform

Your website is an asset. It's the cornerstone of all your marketing efforts and online activity.

Then
Why on earth would we need a telephone?

Now
Why on earth would we need a website?

Your website: The mother ship

Lots of things will happen as you move along. You may try blogging, social media or whatever is invented 2 years from now, but everything needs to link back to one place where you regroup your efforts. This is your website.

Your website is central to your marketing operations. Rather than thinking of it as something you set-and-forget, consider it your online business platform – your **mother ship**. Each activity, piece of content, interaction and marketing effort needs a central hub.

For example, social media may not be your cup of tea, but you could easily prepare and publish an informative eBook on a topic you know lots about. You could easily collect email addresses via your new patient form and use them (with permission) to send special offers to patients so they keep coming back. You can easily set up paid-advertising in Google and Facebook to get qualified leads to call you.

Your online business platform enables you to leverage your knowledge, expertise and passion into a successful practice via a steady stream of clients and systematised marketing.

A good website can help with:

- Getting more visitors
- Better listings in search engines
- Increasing your authority
- Reducing your online advertising costs
- Driving your branding and recognition

- Increasing visitor-to-client conversions
- Getting more repeat business
- Improved patient satisfaction and education
- Getting more referrals from other professionals
- Long-term effects for business

Few businesses understand what their website is really for. The purpose is to develop trust, gain mindshare, and act as a springboard for action. Your marketing and communication activities all need to lead back to your website for conversion and tracking.

For most private practice owners, managing a website goes into the basket of stuff you don't want to do. Having access to good advice and ongoing support can really help with this.

At its core, marketing and business development includes two steps:

1. Lead generation
2. Lead conversion

Lead generation is about online marketing, communications, social media and so on. Lead conversion happens after you have established mind-space in your visitors, built trust, and have a convincing offer or call-to-action.

PracticePulse business platform & ecosystem:

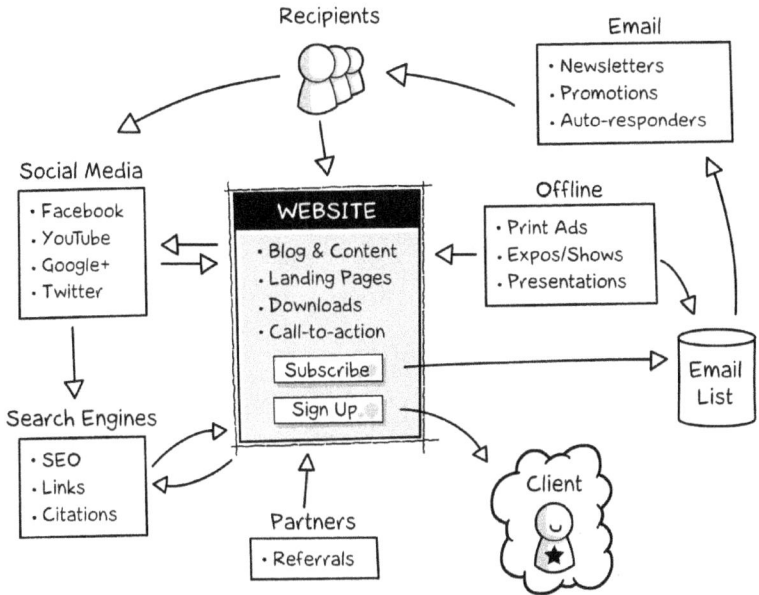

Here you can see how we do things at PracticePulse. This is always changing, as we try out different things. Some other tools we are experimenting with include webinars, seminars, published articles in industry specific journals, guest blogging and of course, this book. It's a lot of work, but this is what it takes in business. Our website, tools and systems make things easier.

Both lead generation and lead conversion have multiple facets and approaches. It's unrealistic to expect that a website alone can do both these things by itself – better websites will help you drive results easier; remember that it's just a tool and you are the driver.

> Everyone needs an awesome website.
> Not every website is awesome.

Lead generation

This is where you reach out to and grab the attention of people who could and would use your services. Traditionally, Yellow Pages and newspaper advertising have been the go-to lead generation strategy.

Nowadays, your website plays an important role in lead generation – if it's set up to do so. Having a good online strategy in place, with a well planned website (mother ship) and a range of activities around it can generate more than enough leads.

Good content, valuable information and satisfying interactions can grab the attention of leads. These can be people who have never visited you before, or existing clients who have forgotten about you.

Simply getting more visitors to your website does not mean you get more leads, however, since you have no means of reaching or communicating with them.

What you really want is for them to hand over their email addresses because they are impressed with what you've displayed and want to learn/see/hear more (or download your eBook, or subscribe to your eNewsletter etc).

Your website must make it easy for a visitor to hand over their email address to you. A "sign up form" is the easiest way to do this. Read more about this in the section on "Email marketing" later in this book.

Lead conversion

Once you've got your leads and are communicating with them regularly, you need to be able to "convert" them into appointments. Your definitive aim is to get someone to see you in person.

There are many ways to do this without turning into that sleazy sales person you're picturing in your mind right now. Remember that if you have grown your email list (leads) via valuable content and interactions, they'll be happy to receive the occasional reminder about why you're in business and what you are offering them.

Traditional marketing is about receiving unwanted phone calls and interrupting people with unwelcome messages that "sell, sell, sell". Most practice owners focus almost exclusively on making the sale. What you're aiming at is "give, give, sell". Becoming an authority in an area gives you more credibility and it means people are more likely to trust you and to come back to see what you have to say, and what you have to sell.

Having enquiry or appointment request forms on your website is a great start, but you can be a lot more proactive than that. Read more about this in the section on "Email marketing" later in this book.

The end result is this: you're reaching out to more people, influencing their health care decisions, helping them to achieve optimum health using your knowledge and experience while growing your business at the same time.

From this point on, your goal must be to generate leads first then focus on conversions. Turning visitors into sales is covered in more detail later in this chapter.

> It all starts with your website, as a business platform – your mother ship. Everything else builds on that.

Getting online

Firstly, what does it mean to be "online"? Does it mean having a page within yellowpages.com or some other Internet directory? Does it mean having a Facebook Page for your business? Does it mean just having an email address so that people can contact you? Or having a website?

Technically/generally speaking, any one of these puts you "online". The question is, how online do you need to be?

In 1996, there were about 100 thousand websites on the Internet. In 2013 this number is around 700 million. In Google's first official year (1998), there were less than 10 thousand searches conducted per day. Now it's in excess of 3 billion. In the last 12 years, the number of emails sent in a day has risen from 31 billion to 300 billion. I won't even get started about the rise of social media.

Nowadays, if a practice owner thinks that a website isn't necessary for their business, it's probably because:

1. They have been burnt in the past with some bad advice or implementation.
2. They haven't seen what a well-executed online strategy can do for their practice.
3. They operate a local business and everyone in their town knows them anyway.

Since you picked up this book, chances are I don't need to sell you the premise that you need to be online. There are a few things I'd like to cover here in any case, to set the pace and context of this book.

Online presence and "buzz" are typically associated with "global reach". As a private practice servicing a limited geographic radius, you may think, "what good is that to me?" and you'd be absolutely right. If you were a physiotherapist or a chiropractor in a rural town in Australia, you wouldn't care to reach someone with back pain in Johannesburg, South Africa.

Your services can't be fulfilled online or by post – you and your clients/patients will always need to meet in person at some point.

There's so much more to an online presence than simply its inherent reach, and much of what it offers are invaluable tools in the right hands.

At this point, let's clarify that "online presence" means being found online. At its core it generally refers to a practice website, but it also covers things like online directory listings (specific to your industry), social media sites (such as Facebook) and professional networks (such as LinkedIn) – even just email. It means that you can be looked up and contacted via the Internet.

Q: Why do you need to be online?
A: That's where your clients are.

The first place people turn to for information today is the Internet. It's the fastest growing and biggest source for information. Whether it's to compare dishwashers or self-diagnose a pain in the knee, a few simple queries in Google will generally reveal as much information as one can handle. Searching for health related information is among the most popular uses of the Internet today.

This unprecedented access to information has created empowered consumers; it has also set expectations that businesses of all sizes be online. If your online presence does not have a place in the user's search results at the time they are searching for something you offer, then you may as well not exist.

Empowered and savvy users also know how to find stuff. As an Internet user, you may search for "back pain" and get a million suggestions in Google. However, (going back to our previous example) if you are in Johannesburg and want a remedy, the search query would probably be refined as "back pain relief Johannesburg". This makes sense since you want someone local to treat you. Whilst a chiropractor or physiotherapist in rural Australia won't care much about such a query, a practice in Johannesburg would definitely be interested in a hot lead.

A Harris survey conducted in January 2011 on behalf of Insider Pages, an online directory that has a "physician finder", found that most people look for physicians based solely on their location.

> The local reach of the Internet is just as significant as its global reach.

A well-maintained online presence is smart business decision. Reliance on great physical location near hospitals or busy shopping areas in your town is no longer sufficient. Neither is reliance on that quarter-page Yellow Pages advert that cost you a ton and got seen by 3 people. If your clients can't find you online, they may as well go to one of your competitors. At a minimum, you need to be found when someone searches for you by your business name in Google.

As online media consumption continues to increase, traditional media continues to plummet. People are spending more time on their smartphones and tablets and less time with TV and newspapers. You've surely noticed your printed Yellow Pages books getting thinner in recent years!

Besides the client expectation to be online, businesses are realising the dynamism and accountability that a good online presence offers when it comes to sales and marketing.

It's possible to quickly determine what your target market is interested in simply by measuring their reaction to your online actions. You no longer need to wait a whole year to try something different with your next Yellow Pages advert. Your websites provides endless avenues for marketing and advertising campaigns as well as establishing credibility, loyalty and a professional appearance. Getting personal with your target market, building and nurturing relationships online is easy and practical.

Online is also a great place for you to gain authority and show public responsibility as a health professional. An abundance of available information means self-diagnosis of various conditions at generic information websites by the public can lead to dangerous consequences. Through a planned online strategy, you can provide the right information at the tight time – building trust on autopilot and ensuring that you remain at the front-of-mind when you are needed.

Your new practice website

Getting online with a website, managing it and updating it can be as easy or difficult as you want to make it. There are so many options available, each with its advantages and disadvantages.

As you'll find out in this book, you need to grasp several concepts so that you can decide on a strategy, and then you need to plan a rollout of your strategy before actually getting something made. This is just ensuring that your ladder is leaning on the right wall before you start climbing.

Your needs and goals

Firstly, you need to be clear on why you want a website. Is it simply to meet the expectations of your clients without much input or intervention from you (i.e. be found online in the most basic form)? Do you want to reach key referral sources? Do you want to generate a pipeline of leads, enquiries and appointments? Do you want to be recognised as an expert in a certain field or specialist area?

At this stage, don't worry about specifics, such as design and branding, blogs, galleries, online forms, content etc. These will be introduced later in this book and will form your strategy based on your client demographics and your own strengths or interests.

Then you need to consider how much time and effort you will be able to input during the initial setup and then the ongoing maintenance and upkeep. Just like anything else, more you put into something, the more you get out.

Your needs and goals may change over time – that's OK. You just need a starting point and a benchmark to measure your results. With a good website and some good support, you'll be able to quickly and easily adapt to changes.

Start by defining your website needs and goals. Your web developer will be able to guide you and help determine these.

Your strategy

So we've established that people will look you up online and expect to find you. They'll judge you based on your presence and their experience. Their experience will be guided by what you offer, how well you understand them and their needs and demonstrating your ability to address their needs. Remember, people online are impatient (even you; not willing to go the extra click or wait the extra 15 seconds for a page to load).

They'll make snap decisions based on what they immediately see about you – whether it's your website or reviews left by other users about you. So how can any responsible practice owner leave any of this to chance?

Your strategy will depend on three things:

1.   Your needs (as above)
2.   Your target demographic
3.   Your strengths or interests

You may find that your target demographic is highly tuned to social media (especially a younger age bracket). A part of your strategy may target doctors specifically for referrals. Or elder citizens may constitute the majority of your client base. Your strategy will need to take these into consideration.

Your strengths are also important. If you find that social media is too daunting or time consuming and there's nothing that can persuade you to pursue it, then you'll need to develop a different strategy. You may find that shooting short informative videos are fun and easy – great! You can surely leverage that!

You'll be surprised to see that there are cost effective solutions available for just about any strategy. So don't allow a salesperson to sell you something before you understand what you're buying. Much of the time it could be something you can do yourself or on the cheap.

Your physical location will also play an important role in your strategy.

> You should always feel free and comfortable discussing this with your web developer. They're there to help.

These are all covered in this book. And remember; your strategy need not be fixed. It's easy to try new things online, so you should be trying different things to see what works for you – be dynamic, not static. Also remember that the Internet is a landscape that is ever-changing – who knows, a year or two from now, there may be completely new tools and services available to you. Once you feel empowered and confident, you'll be comfortable in trying these out.

Don't be shy

Once you have a website, plaster your domain name everywhere you can think of. This includes your adverts, letterheads, business cards, signage, social media pages, email signatures and wherever else you can think of.

When you set up a social media profile (e.g. Facebook and Google+), you should include URLs for these too.

Do you already have a website?

If you're the only provider in your local area and your website was created with some forethought, it may be enough meet your needs without much intervention or upkeep. You may simply need a few basic updates occasionally, like changed business hours, staff details or photos. Having a website with out-dated information, timetables, fee listings or contact details is an absolute no-no. Remember – your competition wants your clients.

Check the following:

- Can the average user find your website in Google, when they search for your practice by name?
- Can the average user find your website in Google, when they search for the services you offer locally? (E.g. Pilates Carlton, back pain Ontario)
- Is your website address easy to remember and spell?
- For visitors who are ready to buy from you, is it easy for them to locate your contact details, enquiry forms and location map?
- Is your website design attractive, suitable and easy to navigate?

- Are you able to make updates to your website content yourself or do you have access to someone who can do it for you?

- How difficult is it for you to try new things on your website? (e.g. start a blog, embed a YouTube video, link up with social media, showcase testimonials etc.)

- Do you have good, engaging or educational content on your website to help convert visitors who aren't quite ready to buy from you yet?

- Are you able to collect email addresses for the purpose of sending e-newsletters? Are you able to write and send e-newsletters?

- Do you have email addresses using the same domain as your website or are you stuck using free services such as Hotmail or Gmail?

- Are you able to measure how many people are visiting your website and what they're doing while they're there? Do you know what's working and what's not?

Consider starting over

Sometimes, if a website was built with forethought, it's not very difficult to simply tweak and fine-tune it with the things you need done. Of course, this may mean that you will need the help of a technical person who understands what needs to be done and can also guide you in implementing your ideas. Simple content updates are something that almost any web developer can do.

However, the fact is, in many cases, starting over with a new strategy is easier and more cost effective than trying to retrofit an existing website with new functionality.

After reading this book and finding out about all the different options you have and determining what you want your website to be (and do), chances are you may want to start over.

A website re-design can become a dangerous venture if you're not re-designing for the right reasons. Consider the right reasons why you would want to redesign your website:

- You want your website to be found by more prospects (better visibility)
- You want to convert more of these prospects into clients (better performance)
- Your existing website does not make it easy for you to grow it or try new ideas; trying to retrofit it just turns it into a bigger monster (better adaptability)
- You want to improve your authority, branding and image, as long as this ties in with any of the other reasons above.

Sometimes, the business owner wants to redesign simply because she/he is tired of the way it looks. This is never a good reason.

Redesigning a website is not a decision to be made lightly, especially if your existing website already has a lot of "Google good-will". When starting over with a new website, you don't want to throw the baby out with the bath water and lose your existing rankings based on content that was indexed by Google. Make sure your new web developers are on the ball when it comes to this.

More about search engines later in this book.

> Don't damage any of your existing website's presence and value
> already created with Google rankings.

Multiple websites for multiple locations

As discussed earlier, your practice serves a localised group of
people; you reach a certain radius around your practice. Unless
you're a specialist surgeon, it's generally not likely that someone
will come to you specifically, from another state.

So this introduces an interesting question. What if you have more
than one location? Do you need multiple websites?

If your clinics serve an overlapping target client base, then you
can probably get away with a combined website. Just make sure
that you clearly indicate your different locations, their addresses
and contact details. It's worth considering setting up separate
pages within your website for each location.

However, if they're geographically so far apart that clients are
likely to prefer going to one or the other, or you offer differing
services at each clinic, then you should consider using separate
websites.

Having separate websites has the advantage in that each website
URL (domain name) can be better suited to the locations (more
about domain names later) and each website's content can be
better optimised for improved rankings in search engines based
on its location.

Your domain name

Your domain name is your address on the Internet. It's the yourname.com. Having your own domain name is crucial for a professional online presence.

Technically, the "www" portion is not a part of the domain name, but it is commonly used with the domain name for a website.

Domain names are registered (purchased) through organisations known as "registrars". Some registrars also offer other services, such as hosting and email accounts. Services such as these are essentially attached to your domain name.

Your domain name enables someone to visit your website by simply typing it into a web browser (like punching your number into a phone). It also allows you to get email accounts on your domain (such as john@yourname.com).

Types of domain names

Most domain names end in .com. These extensions generally denote the country of operation for a business. For example, Australian businesses would opt for a .com.au domain.

It's highly recommended to use a domain name suited for the country you're in. The public has general awareness and familiarity with the local domain names and will associate with them easily.

Eligibility

Some extensions have special eligibility criteria. For example, before you can register a .com.au domain name you need to be able to prove to the registrar that you're an Australian entity and the domain name you seek is closely linked to your business name or service offering. This type of regulation helps protect businesses from having domain names being purchased and held hostage. There have been many legal cases where a company or individual has registered a domain name solely for the purpose of selling it to a rightful business or abusing it. Imagine if someone from Dominos was able to register the domain pizzahut.com.au – you can see things getting ugly.

The common .com type domain names have no restrictions or eligibility criteria.

Choosing a good domain name

It's important to choose a good business name for your practice; a domain name should be selected with as much careful thought. Your domain name plays an important role when people search for, discover, explore, talk about and remember a website. It establishes who you are before people even visit your practice website for the first time.

Note that your ideal domain name may not be the same as your business name. Here are a few tips to keep in mind, when brainstorming for the perfect domain name:

Use the correct type

Avoid anything with .net or .org – these are generally not associated with businesses like private practice.

Include keywords

You should try to include your primary service in your domain name. Most likely there are such keywords in your business name already. Including words such as these not only aids in making your domain name easy to remember, it also helps set visitor expectations before they arrive at your website.

Another inclusion should be your location – generally your suburb (or town) name. Including this in your domain will help with search engine placements later on. It'll also make it easier for local people (who are your target prospects) to remember your domain name.

Keep it simple

If you've had someone spell out a website address to you over the phone or you've tried reading it off a sign while driving, you'll know that simple is best. If it rolls off the tongue and pronounces well, it'll likely be remembered.

Avoid domain names similar to that of your competition; otherwise you risk losing visitors to the competition's website – especially if that website is well established.

Availability

It's no good deciding on a domain name if it's already taken by someone else. Registrars will have tools for you to check the availability of a domain name, before allowing you to register it.

> If you are stuck for ideas or unsure of which domain name would work best for your practice, get in touch with your web developers.

An example:

Let's assume your practice is called "Drew McMahon Chiropractic" (named after you), practicing out of Essendon in Victoria Australia and specialising in treating back pain.

Firstly, you would opt for a .com.au extension. Secondly, you would consider your services and location – this is more important for search engine placements going forward, than your business (or personal) name.

Here are some good domain name ideas:

- essendonbackpainchiro.com.au
- backpainessendon.com.au
- essendonchiro.com.au

These indicate what you offer and are easy to remember. Here's a bad domain name, unless you are so famous that people search for you specifically by name:

- drewmcmahonchiropractic.com.au

Note that you can register more than one domain and choose one as your "primary domain" for your website. This would prevent other businesses registering similar domain names and diluting your domain's stickiness.

Registering a domain name

There are many registrars, with whom you can register your domain name. You can find suitable registrars simply by searching in Google for "domain name registrar" or "register a .com.au domain" etc.

Most registrars are very straightforward and easy to navigate. However some are notoriously difficult, as they try to up sell you a dozen other services that you will never need. If in doubt, ask your web developer to recommend a registrar or handle the registration for you.

After it is registered, you need to renew it – typically every one or two years. If you do not renew your domain name, it will expire and after a grace period, it will be available on the market for someone else to register. If you use correct contact information when you register your domain name, you will receive an email reminder when your renewal date approaches.

Prices

Prices for domain name registrations differ from one registrar to the next. At this time, .com domains are going for around $8-$15 per year. Country specific domains are more expensive. Compare prices at a few registrars' websites to get a feel for the market.

Scams

There are companies out there who try to sell you domain names that you don't need. They typically approach you via email or even post, with a message that sounds like this:

"Hello ABC Chiropractic. We note that the domain abcchiro.co.in has become available – if you don't register it immediately, it can be taken by some other company and used without your permission. Contact us to register this domain name immediately".

Firstly, be clear on what they are trying to sell you – in this case a domain name with the extension ".co.in" – typically for Indian businesses. Do you really care to get this domain name? Especially when you note that these guys are asking you to pay 3 times the going rate?

Scams prey on business owners' ignorance, by creating a sense of urgency. If in doubt, contact your web developer.

Hosting

Now that you have your domain name, it needs to be pointed to some web and email servers. "Servers" are simply stacks of computers that sit in a large data-centre that are responsible for "hosting" your website and email accounts.

Your domain name and hosting work hand in hand to deliver your website to the world. Setting all this up is the responsibility of your web developer – you needn't worry about any of this. Point to take away, though, is that your domain name and hosting service are separate things and can be handled by different companies. You may pay separate fees for your domain name renewals and your hosting account.

Email accounts

Just like your website files are hosted on a server, your email accounts are also provided by servers. When someone sends an email to you@yourname.com, the email is received by your mail server and stored there to be picked up when you are ready.

Email accounts from the likes of Hotmail and Gmail should be avoided for business use. You now have your own domain name, so go ahead and look more professional by using an email account on your own domain.

Security and spam

Spam is a fact of life. We all hate it, but we've learnt to live with it. Fortunately, most hosting companies' email servers have built in spam detectors so that most (if not all) never makes it into your inbox. Some spam may still slip through.

A bigger problem than spam is when you receive suspicious attachments from hackers and other people of ill intent. Some attachments are disguised as legitimate documents, which you are urged to open. Sure enough, they contain "malware" or a virus which can go onto damaging your computer or stealing information.

Email is a very common transport method for malware and viruses. Ensure you are protected with good anti-virus software.

Looking good

Take a guess... how long do you think the average person take to form a first impression about you and your practice upon landing on your website? Numerous studies indicate that this figure is a fraction of a second. What first impressions do you give through your website? These first impressions carry through their time on your website (if they stick around) and affect their judgement as to whether they'll seek your services or not or whether they return to your website again.

It's simply a trust factor; poor design that looks less than professional with cluttered or unorganised layout will usually lead to a feeling that there could be other areas of your business that are equally poor.

Even if it was subconscious, you've surely had this kind of experience before on other websites!

Who are you designing for?

First thing to remember is that you are not designing for you—you are designing for prospects and for your existing clients. Your visitors want and expect different things from different websites. For example, their needs and expectations are different when they are researching an architect online to design their next home, versus a video sharing website where they can find funny clips of cats doing silly things.

On your business website a simple, clean and professional design with a concise message will improve the ease of use for your prospects and allow them to find exactly what they're looking for effortlessly. From there, it should be obvious and easy to take the next step, such as contacting you.

> What you and your visitors care for is usually very different. Don't design for yourself.

Remember, it's possible to cater to various needs, such as someone who is after some education about a particular injury as well as someone who needs directions to get to your practice. It just takes some thoughtful planning.

Important design factors

When it comes to design, the foremost important consideration is usability: the user's ability to do what they want to do easily and effortlessly. This accounts for 76% of the "importance" pie. Usability considers things like:

- Intuitive navigation.
- Ability to scan the page for information easily.
- Headlines and titles.
- Ability to tell where within the website they are at any given time.
- Not overwhelming to the user.
- Lightweight design to allow fast loading of the page.
- Good typography and spacing (makes it easier to read).
- Non-distracting images and backgrounds.
- Things simply work as expected.

Next are the aesthetics – how visibly appealing a website is and whether it offers a cutting-edge interactive experience. These rate at 10% and 9% respectively. The remaining 5% accounts for other, less significant factors.

A winning formula

A lot of research has already been done when it comes to what works for website design – regardless of your business and needs.

There are many common elements such as suitability of design, simplicity of layout, placement of logos, menus, social interaction and contact details.

Website designs for businesses in private health practice have a few additional common traits that have been proven to work.

Despite what designers will tell you, it's fine to use pre-made designs. Designs that have been prepared earlier have several advantages, especially if they've been made with your industry's needs in mind:

1. You know exactly what your website will look like (no surprises).
2. Allows for external expertise – the designs have been proven to work, not only with visitors but also with search engines so that they are better at getting indexed and being found.
3. No need to waste time with design briefs and revisions (which can take weeks before your website is even in the build stage)
4. Cost savings – pre made designs cost a fraction of getting a custom website design.
5. Easy to apply a new design later on, when you feel it is necessary to update your image. Design trends come and go – 2 years from now, you should be able to apply a new design easily.
6. If any bugs are discovered in the design, the developer can fix all websites that use that design at the one time. Similarly, if the designer updates the original design to cater for changes in needs, your website would maintain its freshness.
7. Still allows for some flexibility in customising colours and options.

Some disadvantages of pre-made designs are:

1. Your website's design won't be unique (but this isn't important, since your clients are local in nature and a website that looks the same as yours in another state isn't going to be an issue).
2. You are limited to the choices presented and may feel that they don't fully reflect your personal preferences.

I'm an advocate of using professionally prepared designs and strongly believe that most practices can be fully served without going through a full-blown design exercise to create an original design. This will probably get a lot of negative response, especially from web designers who pride themselves on selling custom designs. The important thing to remember is: does your design serve the needs of your visitors and your strategy? If you can achieve this without the additional expense and headaches, why not opt for a pre-made design?

The fastest, easiest and most direct way to a successful website is modelling a formula that works. Don't try to create a custom website design and recreate the wheel, unless your requirements are very specific and you have a ton of cash to throw at design.

This said, there are many pre-made template designs out there that are generated for different industries. Make sure that your chosen design is suitable for your practice.

Must-have pages

At the most basic level, a website should provide clients and prospects with your clinic's contact details, instructions on how to find you and hours of operation. You can also include a description of your services and any registration forms you will require. You can include frequently asked questions, give out free and useful information, and offer to take registrations or appointments online, explain policies and more.

Your website content will obviously be specific to your practice and specialty. When preparing your content, remember to focus on what you can do for your clients, how you can benefit them.

> Keeping the content fresh and updated is also a good idea for visitors to return.

Then you can get into the really powerful stuff, such as communicating and connecting deeply with your clients, marketing intelligently and verifiably with prospects, selling gift certificates and gaining authority while building your brand. Yes, all this is within the grasp of the average practice.

More about content publishing and marketing later.

Homepage

Your homepage is the online face of your practice and your services. You only get one chance to impress your visitors, so make sure you plan what you want them to get on your homepage. It should also act as a launching platform to places where they can contact you or take other action.

When prospects visit your page for the first time they expect to have three questions answered within the first few seconds:

1. Does this website/practice offer what I'm looking for?
2. Does this website/practice appear credible?
3. Do I want to return to this website/practice?

The homepage should contain an introduction to your practice and your major services. Consider for a moment what other content your visitor may want or need. The homepage doesn't need to be heavy with content; you can simply let the user find what they're looking for and provide links to other pages within your website so they can reach them easily.

If you have an introductory video for your practice, your homepage is the place to put it. Just don't make it "auto-play". Keep important stuff near the top of the page so it can be seen without scrolling down the page.

Persistent information

There are some obvious bits of information (or links) that need to be available on every page. These should be placed with consistency and where expected within the page.

> Your telephone number should be at the top of every page, and again at the bottom.

Your address can be in the header (top) of your website, in the footer (bottom) or in a sidebar. The "contact us" link is usually found as the last item of your main navigation menu.

Your logo usually links through to your home page. The first link in your main navigation menu should also be linked to your home page.

Links (or buttons) to your appointment request forms or contact forms should be easily found at all times.

Maps and directions may be embedded somewhere in your sidebar or footer, however, another common practice is to place this information on your contact us page.

Your hours of operation are among the most commonly looked up information. You can place these in a sidebar, footer or on your contact us page.

Unless you're really pushing social media in your practice and business, links to your social media profile pages should be placed discreetly – visitors who are interested will notice them.

If you operate a blog (and you should), a link to your blog should be available prominently – preferably within your main navigation menu.

About your practice

Your "About us" page is very important. You provide health services in your practice – your clients inherently have a more personal relationship with you than they would with the local burger joint.

Visitors to your website will be interested in finding out about you, your staff, practice history and other "about us" stuff. So make sure that you think about this content carefully before preparing these pages.

You can include:

- Your practice history / story
- Who you help
- Staff profiles and qualifications
- Specialist services, benefits, descriptions
- FAQs (frequently asked questions)
- Insurance policies, payment terms, patient intake forms

These can all be categorised and grouped for easy presentation. Don't try to put everything on the one page. In fact, it's a good idea to keep pages short (about 300 words each) and focussed on a key topic. For example, you may consider providing a separate profile page for each staff, grouped under a section called "our staff".

You can also include a page of client testimonies – this is a very powerful way to convert visitors into clients. However, note that there are many regulations in place about doing this sort of thing. Refer to the chapter Ethics and Legal for more information.

Educational material

As we've covered before, health related topics are among the most researched online nowadays. Having content pages that are educational in nature are important to satisfy your visitors' need for information.

You can cover topics such as the different modalities and techniques you use and how these help your clients. You can include pages to inform the public about how you fit in with health services. Research papers (which have been written to be read by the average Joe) can establish you as an expert and authority in your field. You can provide downloadable information sheets and eBooks to your visitors.

Educating your visitors is an invaluable investment for your practice. Educating them reduces many barriers, such as getting them to come in for an appointment, ability to raise your fees and even increasing your referrals from other health professionals.

> Not every visitor will be interested in so much content. However, at minimum, this type of content shows visitors that you have invested in your website and their education – and you know your stuff.

Marketing and promotion

Your website is a business tool. As such, it needs to support your marketing and promotion. Now you may oppose these two words, but this is business; you can't hide from marketing and promotion if you want your practice to thrive.

You need to be able to get website members, i.e. people who have subscribed with their email address, so that you can keep in touch with them. Of course, you'll need to give them an incentive before you can request that they give up their email details to you. These are covered in a later chapter.

To get the most out of your email distribution list, you need to send out newsletters and offers. These can link to a page on your website, created for the sole purpose of displaying your offer. These pages are known as "landing pages" – and they typically contain a great offer. You can later track how many people arrived on that page as a result of your mail-out and also how many people took up your offer.

Images and video

As mentioned earlier, your services are one-to-one, in person. You can't treat someone who is not at your practice. Because of this inherent personal nature of what you do, visitors to your website will want to know who they will be dealing with. Besides reading your staff profiles, photos of your practice and staff are very useful.

Make sure to take good quality photos – they don't need to be professionally shot, but they shouldn't look like a 6 year old took them. Portrait shots with you looking at the camera work best.

Videos are another option to introduce your practice and staff; video communicates with your visitors quickly and effectively. It can also convey the sort of personality that written words can't do justice. It may sound a little daunting to shoot video and put it on your website. You may struggle with the technical aspect of shooting a good video – or your difficulty may lie with being in front of a camera instead. Suffice to say that it's really not difficult, and well worth the time.

Turning visitors into sales

There are several strategies to bring more visitors to your website. However, that's only one half of the equation. Without action, no number of visitors to your website will help your business.

You need visitors to take some desired action, such as:

- Make an appointment online or call your reception.
- Sign up to your newsletter to stay informed.

- Refer you to a friend who may need your services.
- Download an eBook
- Initial engagement (make an enquiry)
- Follow you within social media (e.g. "like" your Facebook page)
- Find your location map, telephone number or other information easily.

Visitors to your website could be at any stage of the buying process. This could range from people who have stumbled across your website by accident and have no need for your services, all the way to "I've made my appointment, I just need your address". Your website needs to be flexible enough to cater for these visitors and everyone in between.

> Granted, only a small percentage of visitors typically take some desired action, however, your website can be optimised to improve your chances.

Clear the path

For the visitors who know what they want from your website, you simply need to clear the path. Here are some tips:

- Provide attractive, uncluttered design.
- Ensure that your appointment request or enquiry forms are easily found. Can your phone number, address, contact page, home page and other important information be found easily at a glance?
- Ensure your website's navigation and layout is consistent throughout.

- Ensure your website loads fast, without large, pointless images.

- Make sure your website is mobile friendly for visitors using smart phones/tablets.

Get attention

Get attention with good headlines and careful formatting. Ensure your content is divided up and presented in digestible chunks. Good headings and useful images go a long way to getting – and maintaining – the attention of visitors. People have a very short attention span online – make it count.

Make them comfortable

Show visitors that you understand their problems and how your services solve them. Do this using their language. Offer good content to showcase your authority. Aim to reduce any friction to making an initial enquiry.

> Photos of your practice, your staff and yourself are great for putting a face to your practice online.

Guarantees & testimonials

Guarantees and testimonials work great in any business. What better way to reduce hesitation and encourage a visitor to make an appointment than a great risk-free guarantee? What better way for someone to feel more comfortable about your services than a list of testimonials from real people whom you've helped in the past?

Public review websites (such as Google+ and Yelp) can be used by anyone to place reviews for any business. Consumers are increasingly using online reviews as a means of making more informed decisions. You may suggest that people leave a review for your practice. However, you MUST avoid any fake or incentivised reviews if you don't want trouble. Reviews and reputation management is covered in more detail later in this book.

One thing to note, while we're at it: your governing bodies or associations may place strict guidelines against guarantees and testimonials. This is covered later in this book.

Call-to-action (CTA)

Recall this from earlier: after getting visitors to your website, the next important goal is to get them to take some desired action.

Sometimes visitors are quite happy to take some action, be it to sign up to your newsletter, or make an appointment with your reception. However, they just need that one last nudge or to clarify any last piece of confusion. Simply telling them what to do next seems too simple, but it's often exactly what your visitors need.

Using explicit instructions with attractive formatting, you can call your visitors to action:

- "Sign up now and receive our free back pain eBook."
- "Discover your ultimate diet. Enter your email here."
- "May I send you a free copy? There is no obligation attached to my offer."

- "Gift one hour massage to a loved one, for half price. Call us now."

> The CTA is like a final instruction to your reader. Don't be shy about it. It's been proven to work wonders over and over again.

Landing pages

Landing pages are especially created to make an offer to readers. They would generally be separate and distinct from your usual website content pages.

Landing pages contain a specific offer, often preceded by sales or marketing spiel and followed by a distinct CTA (call-to-action). It may be set up as a temporary page (which you plan on pulling down after a while), or it may be a permanent page on your website.

A landing page is your opportunity to try different marketing spiels and offers to make a certain sale or get a specific action from visitors. For example, you may create a landing page to promote your new eBook – it could have a video of you talking about your eBook, a list of testimonies from readers (about the eBook), plus a form to capture an email address so that you know where to send the eBook.

You can then point readers to this page with links from your newsletter, blog, social media, home page and more. Having a separate page for such promotions also helps you to track the number of visitors reaching the page and then taking the action. This way you can optimise your future promotions.

> Design compelling landing pages so visitors will be more willing to give away their contact information for your content offerings.

Landing pages should be designed with as little clutter, navigation and distraction as possible. Your offer must be clear, concise and simple (though your sales spiel may be lengthy). As always, use headlines and formatting to get attention as quickly as possible.

Start a relationship

Imagine you have gotten a visitor to your website, grabbed their attention and made them comfortable… But they just don't need you right now. What do you do?

You need a means of staying in touch with visitors – building a relationship with them. You can simply ask them for their email address.

Of course you'll need to do something in return, like offer valuable resources, eBooks, articles, offers and anything else they may want. You'll also need to assure them that their email address will be safe; you won't send them junk, share their email address with anyone else and stop sending them emails when they ask you to. This is known as email marketing and is covered in detail later in this book.

> It all starts with asking for their email address for your list.

Should you sell stuff on your website?

I don't recommend selling physical products via your website because that distracts visitors from your main objective of getting more appointments for the sake of a few bucks profit on a sale. Such online sales have heavy overheads such as inventory control, shipping, tracking. Establishing yourself as a worthwhile eCommerce store is a whole different strategy that takes great effort, coordination, resources and focus. This isn't what you're aiming to do with your practice website.

That said, you can easily sell gift certificates online for general services that anyone can enjoy, such as:

- Massage
- Dental check-up
- Pilates group class
- Health evaluation
- Use of hydrotherapy pool
- Posture evaluation
- Gait analysis

Consider what you can offer as a gift certificate in your business. Think carefully before offering professional treatment, as these may not be suitable or downright disallowed by your governing bodies. The idea is to get people in, having pre-paid for something already.

Selling gift certificates is quite easy to do, and all you need is a PayPal account (which is free to set up) and a means of recording your sales so you can confirm when they are being redeemed. You may want to state an expiration date and enforce advance appointments for redeeming the certificates, especially if they were offered at a discount.

What to avoid on your website

Many bells and whistles have been invented for websites over the years. Most of them have proven to have little (if any) benefit to the average user, and it's about time that website owners dropped these. Here are some examples:

- Flash intros (just noisy and annoying animations that pop up before you enter a website).
- All-Flash websites (Flash is a tool; using it to build your entire website is not a good idea).
- Poor navigation.
- Poor design.
- Irrelevant elements, meaningless graphics.
- Inconsistent styles, colours and fonts.
- Auto-play video and audio (if a visitor wants to see a video, they will click on the play button; don't auto-play videos and leave 80% of visitors looking for the stop button).
- Selling products from your website (it takes considerable effort to bring visitors to your website, hold their attention and convert them into clients; don't distract them with a sale worth a few bucks profit).
- Not providing your contact details (or making visitors scour your website for them).

Building your website

Choosing a web developer

A big mistake is to get a friend to create your website for you or using a "DIY" website system. The problem with going down this path is that you won't have access to the experience and guidance of a seasoned professional. Also, most people who go down this path end up getting stuck in the "nothing ever gets done" game, which I discussed in the previous chapter.

When choosing a web developer (or development agency) check if they are familiar with your industry. Being a private health practice with a focus on local business, you have very specific needs and must pay attention to things that are important to your business.

The problem is that there are so many choices out there... how do you choose someone to help you with your strategy and build your website? Do you choose based on price or do you look at the portfolio of work already done? What will you do when you need support? Will they be there to answer your questions or take care of updates for you? What will happen when your needs change? Will they be around a year or two from now?

Will they help you with your marketing related questions as well or only offer design and development services, leaving you alone to work out the rest? Do they offer complementing services, such as improving your website rankings in search engines?

Are they simply re-packaging existing services or free software and selling it to you for a fee? Yes, this does happen – there are many providers around who "white label" services offered from other companies or website delivery platforms and charge you money for doing very little themselves.

Do you bite the bullet and dish out several thousand dollars up front? Do they offer some form of instalment payment or subscription options? Is there a term contract and if so, are you stuck with it even if they can't deliver on their promises?

There's a lot to think about, and I'm sorry if this makes you more nervous. It's better to know about all this now, than find out later.

When shopping for a web developer (or an agency), ensure that you ask all these questions before you choose one.

> After you've looked at a few providers and have a feel for what your options are, take a look at **PracticePulse.com** – we work exclusively with businesses in private health practice. If you choose not to work with us then be sure not to accept any less from others.

Evolution and growth

Brochure websites are the online equivalent of a printed brochure. They're basically set and forget, never changing, just sitting there. They are relatively cheap to establish, but offer very little value to a practice. Making changes to such a website, or updating it with recent technology is very difficult and costly. You don't want one of these for your business.

You need a website that you can update and manage yourself as required, without having to become an Internet Guru or read through reams of instructions.

Also, what about changing the options and design that's given to you? How much flexibility is there?

So your website strategy should include a means of future-proofing as much as possible. Being stuck with technology that's hard to use, update or maintain is the last thing you want when moving forward quickly is important.

WordPress and other CMS

A Content Management System (CMS for short) will allow you to have a website which can be managed relatively easily. There are many options for this type of website, however, they all have different trade-offs between flexibility, capability, maintainability and usability.

Commonly, a website that has a CMS is sold by web developers as "edit your web pages just like using Microsoft Word." However, that is often half-truth. There's much more you want to be able to do than simply edit the contents of a page. Many CMS packages are very difficult to use when you try to do other stuff on your website (e.g. start a blog, embed a video, integrate with your Facebook page, create a landing page for a new promotion etc.

Some popular and well-established CMS packages are WordPress, Joomla and Drupal. These are all known as "Open Source" which means they are free to obtain and use. For a fee, a web developer would typically customise this free software to suit your design, content and functionality needs, so that the website that runs on this platform works with your online strategy and goals.

CMS packages like WordPress are well established and have extensive support options available. I personally am a fan of WordPress and use it in many personal and business projects. Having said that, however, it's important to note one very significant point about WordPress (and other similar CMS packages): they have been built to be generic in use, meaning that they offer A LOT of functions and features. To get the most out of these with the least frustration, you need a high level of technical skill and expertise.

> As a practice owner (or website administrator), you'll never utilise more than a fraction of what WordPress offers. Everything else simply serves to confuse you and opens the doors for things to go wrong.

For a start, you need to be on the ball with your WordPress security. There are many hackers out there who specialise in breaking into WordPress websites. If you have a WordPress website, you can't afford to "set and forget" it.

There are thousands of pre-made design options and tens of thousands of plug-ins available for WordPress to get it to do even more things. Most of these aren't from reputable sources. This means that extending your website's functionality with new features may introduce a plethora of other problems and security risks. For the average practice owner, WordPress can seem like a mountain to climb.

> Same goes for most other CMS packages. They try to be all things to everyone.

So if brochure websites are no good, and popular CMS packages are overkill, what options do you have? One option is to have your own custom built CMS – however, this is often not viable because of costs involved. It also means you'll be totally reliant on the single web developer who built it for you. It also means that future development and expansion will get even more expensive.

The viable option is to use a web development company who specialises in your industry. For example, at PracticePulse, we've built a platform of website delivery and management, with our own purpose-developed CMS and marketing system.

I've already said that it's not a good idea to rely on a proprietary system. So why am I contradicting myself?

Well, the difference is that in creating our platform, we've looked at hundreds of options and alternatives (including WordPress) to create, deliver and manage websites for our clients. None of them provided enough simplicity, security and focussed feature sets that we wanted our clients to have. Our platform and CMS have also been designed from the ground up to enable our team to support our clients with ease and roll out updates and security patches remotely. Hence our clients' websites always offer the best of what they need, with all the tools built in and unlimited support to boot. As a result, we can also offer our services reliably and at a low cost.

Since we only work with health providers in private practice, we understand our clients intimately and can take all our knowledge and new learning to improve things for all our clients. So our clients win on all accounts.

Check out **practicepulse.com** for more information

Updates and security

Internet technologies are always evolving – as are hackers who'll try to find ways around security measures of a website so they can plaster it with their own (inappropriate) material or steal information from you. If your website is ageing, it may become susceptible to newer forms of hacker attacks. Hence updates and security becomes an important factor of your online strategy.

Disaster planning and recovery

What happens if your website is hacked and plastered with links to shoddy online Viagra stores? OR your hosting company goes bankrupt and your website dies with them? Do you have any backups? Where are they kept and who can restore them quickly?

These are things that you shouldn't need to worry about if you have a reliable and experienced web developer; another reason to go with professionals rather than your nephew who can build websites.

Ongoing support

How often have you purchased some new piece of technology but never fully figured out how to use it? And then one day someone comes by and shows you something seemingly so obvious and you have that "wow!" moment?

Support isn't only important when you're getting started, but also as your website evolves along with your experience and understanding. Who will you call on when you have a new idea that you want to try out? Will someone be around when you need them? Will they respond to you in a timely manner? Will they have experience in consulting businesses like yours? Will they be interested in you and proactively give you tips, ideas or even perform various duties for you?

Good people are hard to find, especially in the technology sector that is renowned for bad service. Remember your last call to your telephone company when you had a query?

When you find good people who speak your language and have your interests front and centre, keep them and use them. Leverage their knowledge and advice.

What will all this cost?

PracticePulse charges a low setup fee, plus affordable monthly service fees that include just about everything you'll need. There are no lock-in contracts so you know you'll get value for your money (otherwise you would take your business elsewhere).

If you want to go down the path of finding an independent web developer or agency, first you need to be sure that they understand your needs both now and in the future. Cutting corners now to save a few bucks can mean much greater expenses in the future when you want to start pushing online possibilities.

A website driven by an open source CMS (like WordPress) can be obtained for as little as a few hundred dollars – if you know what you're doing and are happy to tinker. But for the average practice owner, this isn't realistic. Budget something in the range of $2000 - $4000 for design, configuration and deployment. If you have specific needs with design or functionality, expect to pay more.

Often, the costs are up-front and payable, regardless of whether your website will work for you or not. Then there are your ongoing hosting (discussed earlier) fees to consider – these days you can get reliable hosting for about $20 per month.

You should also budget for updates, maintenance and support. Typically, these cost from $40-$120 per hour, depending on your web developer.

One final consideration: how well does your web developer understand your industry and how proactive are they in pushing to get the most out of your Internet strategy? Do they offer help with content, search engine optimisation, social media advice and education? Are they responsive to your questions or do they treat you like a number?

Setting your expectations

Today's Internet is a very different to what it was even just two years ago. Technology and methods have matured and web users are much savvier. Today, you should expect to generate online leads with your website. You should expect to convert online leads to clients. This should be your primary expectation!

The goal of an effective online strategy for your practice should be

- Attract more visitors
- Convert visitors to clients (lots of visitors is not enough)
- Increase your authority, branding, reputation etc.

- Provide measurable returns on your investment and online activities.

Having a website alone isn't enough to be competitive just as buying a book won't make you a chef. Your website works hand in hand with a lot of other stuff. Like anything too good to be true, "build it and they will come" isn't realistic. Your website is the cornerstone of your online strategy and everything else supplements it. It still needs to be driven, promoted and adaptable to changing requirements and emerging trends.

Remember, your website is a tool. Better tools adapt to your needs and provide better support to get the work done more efficiently. However, you, as the business owner, need to know how to use this wonderful tool. After all, growing your business is still YOUR job. Having good web developers, support and guidance simply makes your job easier and achieves your outcomes with greater effectiveness.

What not to expect

Your website alone will probably not be enough to generate ludicrous amounts of new business referrals; there are many contributors to a good online presence and marketing strategy. However, your website must be the focal point, where everything comes together.

Don't expect your practice website to be a social destination. There are already plenty of websites out there that are very good at these things.

Don't try to emulate the success of another website for a business similar to yours. It's hard to see on the surface what went into creating the success of another website. Your practice, location, client base and many other things are different. Learning the basics and applying your own strategy is a better bet.

Don't expect more traffic than peak hour in Istanbul. You run a local business – you inherently have a limited base of prospects that you can possibly target (i.e. within your geographic reach). Aim to get their attention and be in their minds when they need you. Aim to convert them into clients. Even if you only get few hundred visits a month on your website, as long as you're reaching the right people and your conversions are good, you'll be doing well.

Don't expect to rank at the top of Google immediately. Remember, you're not the only one with that goal; you have competition and there's only one top spot. Especially if your domain name and website are relatively new, expect the process of climbing the search ladder to take even longer than an established website (think months, not weeks).

Don't expect to offload everything onto someone else. Sure, you can get some great help, excellent advice and direction, however, you need to make the ultimate decisions and at least know what's going on with your website and online strategy. Set-and-forget isn't a viable strategy anymore.

Publish: Content creation

There is no market for messages, which is why TV networks have to create programs that you want to watch. Otherwise they would only air commercials.

Importance of content

In terms of marketing your practice, you'll know that most of the traditional activities for getting client attention don't work like they used to. Advertising rarely gets enough response to justify the costs. Asking specialists and referrers for coverage is hard and unreliable. Your brochure website doesn't generate the leads you crave.

You're an expert in what you do and know that there are clients out there who would really value your assistance. How do you attract their interest in this age of noise, spam and short attention spans?

It's the information age. We've already covered how the Internet has changed consumer behaviour. With an abundance and ease of access to information, consumers are looking for answers and advice before they spend their money (even with bricks and mortar businesses). We've also discussed that your business needs to be there, front and centre, when your target consumer is looking for something you can provide.

When they find valuable and relevant information, trust is attributed to its authors. If you're not creating content, you're missing out.

It's worth noting that your clients care about themselves, not your services. Old-school marketing focussing on what you do simply adds to the noise. Therefore, the majority of the information you produce for marketing purposes cannot be about yourself. To build relationships, your material must be based on fulfilling your clients' needs and interests.

Educating your clients, helping them make decisions, giving them valuable tips to achieve successful desired outcomes, demonstrating how you've helped others and answering their questions would all fall under the "useful content" category.

It's easy to share information on the Internet. When someone finds something that's valuable, all they have to do is copy and paste your URL and post it on social media or send it out via email. It takes minimal effort.

> Content marketing: the more you educate them or entertain them, the more they remember you, like you and don't mind being sold to.

Jamie Oliver has created an empire out of content – TV shows, YouTube videos, websites, recipes and more, which are all free. He has gained a massive amount of authority around the world with his initiatives such as Ministry of Food and Jamie Oliver Food Foundation. But he makes his money selling his books, apps and endorsements as a result of the momentum he's gained through his content.

It's the same with you in your practice. What can you prepare, that people value and want, that would get patients or prospects to find you, know you, like you and trust you? Creating and distributing relevant, valuable and compelling content will help you get noticed, trusted and convert prospects into clients and fans of your practice.

Other benefits of content creation include:

- Getting links from other websites (which is important for building up your website profile and search engine positioning).
- Lower price sensitivity for your services (since you're perceived as an authority).
- More referrals and sales (people would rather buy from an affluent expert).
- Puts a human face on your practice.
- Creates greater client loyalty.
- Supports public relations efforts.
- Provides food for social media.

Types of content

For the beginner, content creation is a daunting task. It takes effort and it seems like one of those things that are too hard to manage. However, it's really just a habit that can be cultivated. Simply remembering its importance and setting aside two or three one hour blocks a week can have you pumping out excellent material. It's slow to get started and build and it's something you didn't want to hear when you bought this book – but it's well worth the effort.

Here are some examples of content you can create:

- Educational articles
- Blog posts
- Videos
- Newsletters
- Well prepared eBooks
- Tips and advice
- Online training programs

- Information sheets, digital brochures
- Reference charts and guides
- Infographics
- Guest posts on other blogs
- Podcasts
- Research papers
- Forum discussions
- Printed books

There are eBooks and blog posts I wrote years ago that still pop up regularly in search engines and drive qualified leads to PracticePulse.

What makes good content?

When done badly, content can be a waste of your time. The concept of "good content" is subjective, and creating it requires forethought and practice. Here are a few guidelines, from a reader's point of view:

- Would you trust the information presented?
- Is it written by someone who knows the topic well?
- Is it driven by genuine interests of readers?
- Does it provide substantial value?
- Does it contain insightful analysis or interesting information that's beyond obvious?

The key to creating valuable, meaningful content for your visitors is to understand their needs and wants, not what you want to stuff down their throats. Consider people who have no knowledge or experience about what you do or how you can help them. Then consider existing clients or patients who want insights and expert tips. You can simply ask existing clients what they want. You can also ask them about their decision making process when they came to see you. By asking questions, you can get interesting perspectives on the people you are trying to reach.

> Approach content creation from the point of view of "How can I help?" instead of "Look how smart I am."

If you have significant traffic on your website, you can use website analytics to determine usage patterns and the types of information that is most viewed. Analytics is covered later in this book.

You can even simply ask your receptionist what the most common questions or the strangest questions are to start building up some ideas about your content roadmap. Prepare content that people are already looking for. You can always introduce more detailed topics through these.

Once you have a few clear profiles of your visitors, you can start thinking about the types of content they'll want. Think "How do I get them in, how do I demonstrate my value to them? How do I educate them to make better choices about their health?"

The next step is to plan out the content you could produce based on your knowledge and expertise. You could share specific experiences, provide actionable advice and differentiate yourself from your competition.

> The goal is not simply to produce content. It's also to give people something useful, entertaining, interactive or all of the above.

Keep a list of ideas

It can be satisfying to write about something you are intimately knowledgeable of. If you're a natural writer, you could just sit down and start. However, planning your topics and giving them some structure will help.

Having nothing to write about is a barrier to regular content creation. Keeping a list of ideas is a great way to overcome this. I get my best ideas in bed and in the shower (not just for writing, but pretty much everything in my life). If I don't write it down, I will surely forget it and later kick myself trying to remember.

Whenever you have an idea, simply add it to your list. Then scan your list and see if it would help to organise them so you know at a glance which topics are high priority, or which topics could go well together.

A running list of ideas will help you group your topics and achieve a wider coverage across different mediums too. For example, your list may suggest that you prepare a multi-part video series with accompanying downloadable summary sheets, which you can then leverage with references in your newsletters and blog posts.

There are many ways to keep a running list; even a text file or Word document will suffice. I use an online to-do list. I can add ideas using my smartphone at any time they come to me.

Content originality

"Creation" means to produce or craft – not just copy something someone else has done. Remember, you want to add value so you need to be original with your content.

Just about every topic under the sun has already been covered by someone. Original content does not necessarily mean something that has never been written about or recorded in video. What matters is that you add value – offer your own version, based on your own expertise and experience, in a way your own readers would benefit.

When it comes to health services within private practice, there are obvious standardised topics and discussions. For example, adjustments in chiropractic, ultrasound in physiotherapy etc. There are only so many ways one can write about these. There is plenty of good content you can simply link to, or public domain content libraries you can utilise. This is fine to use as long as your clients and website visitors find these beneficial and they don't infringe copyright laws.

However, real value and authority comes from the material you produce yourself within your practice, in your own voice. Even if this is nothing more than linking to an existing article and discussing your opinions and experiences around it.

> Creative and original content is the most powerful way of attracting and retaining website visitors. Create content so valuable that it shares itself.

Write for your readers

Remember who your readers are; they haven't been educated in your field. The things you consider common sense are generally a total mystery to your readers. Don't assume they know anything. Your jargon and tech-speak will be foreign to them; don't be afraid to dumb things down too far. Aim to be understood by an average teenager. This applies to everything, from your website, to emails, to YouTube videos.

People have very short attention spans. Confusing your audience with complex, industry jargon is a good way to alienate. You should write conversationally and aim to be understood. People generally write differently to how they talk (e.g. sign off an email with "Best Regards, Joe"). This is just a habit. Don't get fancy – writing as though you are talking with someone helps build rapport and trust.

Your great new content needs to be easily scanned with lots of headings, subheadings, spacing and bullet points. Use of selective formatting (like bold and italic), simple colour scheme and good images will help to hold interest.

> You're a practice owner, a business person, an entrepreneur. No one quite expects you to be a prize-winning novelist.

Getting others to write

It makes most sense for you (as the practice owner or the person with the highest profile in your business) to build authority and trust through your writing. However, there's no reason why you couldn't have other "contributors" to share your workload. This helps you with the writing workload and it could introduce fresh perspectives and voices to your readers.

Here are some examples:

- Get a guest blogger with specific expertise to write a post on your blog

- Have a team member's "corner" in your regular newsletter.
- Conduct (and transcribe) an interview with an expert.

Hiring a content creator

Since building authority and trust is the aim, hiring an external resource to produce content for your practice is probably not a good idea. You want authentic content that has your personality all over it.

That said, if you need someone to write marketing-focussed material, you could always bring in a professional. Whatever you do, make sure that it's driven by your overall strategy – the tone, style and quality must match your clients' expectations. Invest in some realistic "test" jobs before deciding on an external writer.

Also note that you will be responsible for ensuring that the content you "purchase" is original and suitable. If you run into copyright issues later, it'll be you held accountable, not the writer.

Integrating sales

Providing a ton of valuable and sought-after content is one thing. It gets attention, builds relationships and makes sales easier. But the sales still need to be made. Referring back to the section on lead conversion, you need to find a balance and push sales too. After all, you're in business and this is a fact you can't forget.

If you're offering value in your content, it's fine to add a call-to-action; whether it be to pick up the phone to make an appointment, leave an email address for further education and marketing, or refer someone to your business. A common mistake is to make the call-to-action either too weak or exclude it altogether. Your reader has gotten to the bottom of your article or end of your eBook or last frame of your video – obviously it was valuable for them. Fill them in on how YOU can help them further. They have a problem; you have the solution.

Remember, balance is key. Make it win-win.

Content distribution

Content itself is no good in isolation. It needs to be distributed to be seen and appreciated. Your website is a great place to start. People want to do business with those they know, like and trust. Getting your content out and reaching as many people as you can and as often as you can is the next task.

Be prolific

People tend to develop a preference for things simply by being exposed to them regularly. Familiarity with something develops trust and likeability. This is why big brands continue to spend massive amounts of money on advertisement.

Your content has more chance of being consumed and remembered if you can get it in front of more people, more often and in more formats.

One article or eBook is not enough to establish you as a thought leader or an expert and develop engagement. You need to be committed to the process of regular creation. You need to prolific.

> You need to be prolific, not perfect. Get your stuff out there.

There are always opportunities to extend your reach by leveraging your content across different channels and mediums. For example:

- You can include a summary of your new eBook in a blog post and monthly newsletter. Don't forget to add a link to a page where it can be downloaded.
- Post status messages in your social media channels with links to your content at your website. Highlight why people should come and see it.
- Print out pages from your website and put them up at your reception for people to take home.
- Look for discussions in public forums about an article you've already written. Invite people to view and discuss your thoughts.
- Use your content as your pitch for speaking gigs.
- Use speaking gigs as an opportunity to get people to your website and view your other content.
- Link to relevant content when you are commenting on other online articles and blog posts.
- Offer your local newspaper a cut-down version of your recent eBook.
- Encourage your readers to distribute these further simply by sharing within their own social media networks.

You've already done the hard work – now get it out there.

Be found online

There are two main ways to deliver the content you create on the web. Being prolific and distributing to as many channels as possible is the first. This takes effort.

The second, however, ideally develops organically: search engines are good at finding good content when people are looking for it. How much your content is aligned with the search terms and conditions, and how reputable you are in the search engines' eyes basically determine how well your content (or website) ranks.

Your service solves a problem and people are actively looking for solutions online. Remember that the public often needs to be educated about the benefits of your service. They may not think of searching for your services, but they sure will be researching their symptoms and problems online, for which YOU could have prepared some content about.

There's a whole section later in this book on search engines. In short, search engines notice when you create loads of valuable and original content. They also notice when people start talking about you and/or your content within their social circles online.

As your online presence grows with your content creation activities, you will enjoy the snowball effect.

Your practice blog

Among the various types of content you could produce for your practice online, blogging is probably one of the most effective when it comes to demonstrating leadership and authority, improving search engine results, building relationships, educating readers, communicating news and turning leads into clients. A blog also gives your company a means of showcasing its personality and culture.

Let's start with the obvious question most of you are asking. What exactly is a blog?

A blog is derived from "web log". In the early days, some people discovered how easy it was to get content up on the Internet and started posting regular logs of their activities, thoughts, ideas and ramblings on a website they built for this purpose.

Today, a blog is basically an online publication platform. It's comprised of "posts" which are individual articles with a headline (title), description, date-stamp and content. These posts are generally listed in reverse chronological order as a "blog roll", so that the latest posts are easily accessible. They may also be categorised so that readers can access other posts listed under similar topics.

Let's use your favourite newspaper column as an analogy. Imagine going to all the back issues and cutting them all out. Now list them in order so that today's article is at the top. You basically have a blog roll. All the "posts" are related to a certain theme of interest, whether it be world news, technology, chess strategy or parenting; this is why it's your favourite column. After reading a headline and description, you can click through and read the whole post. But what makes it really valuable for you is that you can search and access all the back-issues quickly and find related posts without having to buy the whole newspaper. You can also share an interesting post easily with friends.

Just like newspaper columns, blog authors have a specialised area of expertise, certain style of writing and know their readers. The posts don't need to be very long (in fact, about 400 words is optimum) and they encourage feedback and discussion. They aim to regularly educate or offer value in order to build up a following.

A blog can be presented as a stand-alone website (where the whole website is the blog), or it can form a portion of another website (i.e. click on a menu item to read the blog roll). In any case, it has the potential to form a large portion of your content creation and inbound marketing strategy (covered later in this book).

Why should you blog?

Your practice blog serves several purposes:

- Position you as an expert and build your authority.
- Allows the personality of your practice to come through – people buy from people, not businesses.
- Connect with influencers and referrers.
- Generate leads.
- Become a better researcher, writer and speaker.
- Provide social proof that services offered at your practice work.
- Provide keyword-rich content for search engines to index and external websites to link. These help raise your profile in search results.

- Encourage regular readership, audience engagement and interactivity.
- Leverage content for packaging as eBooks, social media sharing or other products.
- Get your ideas in order.
- Show that your practice is active.
- Help maintain your online reputation.
- Low cost marketing.

If these benefits haven't convinced you to start blogging, note that companies that blog regularly get 55% more visitors, 88% more leads, 97% more inbound links from other websites and 434% more indexed pages in search engines[1]. The number of leads generated online increase significantly as a business' blogging activities are ramped up. More than 30% of companies report their blog as a factor influencing purchases. Blogs outrank social networks for consumer influence[2].

If you are hesitant, it's probably because:

- You think it's a big job.
- You don't think anyone will care to read your blog.
- You don't like to experiment.
- You don't feel comfortable putting yourself out there.
- You don't know what to blog about.

These don't change the fact that blogging forms a major portion of Internet marketing and profile building – and it's still on the

---

[1] HubSpot, 100 Awesome Marketing Stats, Charts and Graphs for You, 2011
[2] Technorati Media's Digital Influence Report, 2013

rise. Yes, it's a big commitment, but there are ways to make your job easier. Yes, initially there won't be many readers (but search engines will index your posts nevertheless). Plus, one single post you wrote may be the sole reason a new client has decided to come see you.

If you're not blogging already, and you have the capabilities to do so, you should seriously consider it. Blogging is something you can learn and get very good at in a relatively short period of time.

How to start a blog

Once you've decided to start blogging, you need to set up your blog.

It's important to note that technically, a blog is simply a website that has special features and functions. It's a website that helps you add content and offers tools to make your blogging activities simpler.

There's no need to get into much technical detail here; in any case, it's likely that you'll need the assistance of a web developer to establish your blog properly. There are numerous free options around such as Tumblr, Blogger, Medium and Typepad – however, these are more suited for personal bloggers and you would be advised to create a lasting setup within your own website for a number of reasons such as:

1. You can manage your practice website and blog via the same interface.
2. Search engine goodwill that your blog builds carries over to the rest of your website.

3. Your branding, familiar design elements and common calls-to-action (e.g. newsletter signup form) are consistent and can be managed centrally.
4. You can better track visitor behaviour as they move between your website pages and blog posts.
5. You don't need separate domain names or hosting accounts.

You may have heard about WordPress; a free to obtain and it can run your website and blog together. WordPress is a good option – it does many things really well. However it can be quit daunting and become a nightmare to manage. WordPress and other CMS were covered earlier in this book.

PracticePulse websites include blog features and are pre-tuned for most private practice needs, avoiding the need for complex settings and external plug-ins. You can simply start posting without any help.

What do you say?

When getting started, deciding on what to say is a big barrier. First thing to do is to decide on your blog's business objectives. Do you want to build your brand? Expand your reach? Support sales? Build authority?

Secondly, consider your audience and what they'll be interested in. Most bloggers have developed a list of topics and planed their posts in advance. Here are few ideas to get you started generating your blog topics:

- Tips: general wellbeing, saving time, maintaining a routine, preparing for an appointment, managing pain etc. So many possibilities right here.

- Why something works (or doesn't work).
- How to be/do/have something.
- Dispel myths.
- Answer common questions.
- Behind the scenes look at your practice.
- Recent research and developments in your field.
- Clarify common issues and misconceptions.
- Explain or clarify industry information.
- Break news.
- Book reviews of industry-specific publications.

Here are some popular blog post formats – see which one feels easiest for you to get started.

Narrative post: Basic article, story or event coverage.

List: Quite easy to write, consisting of a list of references, ideas, to-dos, Q&A etc. Think of posts that begin with "Top 10" or "7 ways to". These are easy for readers to consume too.

Opinion: Your personal opinion, rave or rant. These are great for generating buzz, comments and polarising discussions.

Referencing post: Introduces another post somewhere on the Internet and provides commentary or opinions. Includes a link to the original post.

Multimedia: You are not limited to text. Sometimes referred to as a vlog (video log), getting in front of a camera and recording your post is a great way to get it into your blog. Embedding video into a post is easy. These are effortless for your audience to view.

Blogging tips

There are several ways to minimise the work you put into your blog and maximise your results. However, don't forget that it takes time and practice to become a good writer and build a following.

Develop your voice

Remember – people write blogs, not the business or the practice. You're expected to have your own informed and biased opinions and let your personality shine through. Be compelling and personal – discuss topics like you would with someone in person. Avoid jargon, filler words and corporate-speak. Aim to be understood by a teenage reader.

Feel free to tell your story, put a face to your practice. Skip the same old thing that everyone else is doing. Remember that being personable and informal doesn't mean underselling your expertise – it shows that you know your stuff. Readers must be able to trust you. Being informal also doesn't mean you can use poor spelling and grammar.

Writing your posts

Ensure that your posts are original. The topic may have been written about a million times before but your post needs to be YOURS. Don't just reword someone else's post. Be insightful beyond the obvious.

Watch out for spelling and factual errors. Errors slip through easily enough. Review your content before posting it.

Remember that you can use images, charts, graphics, video and audio recordings in your posts. Feel free to mix it up and use media other than text to convey your thoughts.

Drive your topics by genuine reader interest and value – not because it would rank well in search engines. Stay on topic within your post and in context within your blog. Cross-link to other posts or web pages (either on your website or others) so your readers can explore topics further.

Format

- Keep your posts to about 500-700 words. Break up large topics if necessary.
- Use clear, attention grabbing headlines
- Use subheadings and bullet points abundantly. Make your post scannable quickly.
- Use short sentences and paragraphs.
- Add a relevant and appropriate image to your post. It's worth finding such an image.

Regularity

Aim for few posts a month.

> Frequency is important, but regularity will help build a following.

Search engines also favour and index your website more often if it has a history of regular updates.

With most blogging systems, you're able to upload several posts in advance and schedule them to be pushed live at given dates. This avoids the need to sit down each week and write.

Planning your posts

Coming up with new ideas and post topics is hard. Keeping a list of ideas was covered earlier in this chapter. You may want to develop some focussed categories. You can grow your blog post ideas list as ideas come to you. You might find that certain posts get a lot of attention. Maybe new research has become available in your field. Perhaps your practice and staff got involved with a local community event. There are always new topics you can write about.

Having a list of topics is great when it comes time to sit down and write. You can organise your topics and plan out a roadmap of the content you want to cover over the coming months.

It's easier then to set aside time and write a few posts in the one sitting and then schedule them to be pushed live at intervals over the coming month. Consider using a basic calendar to publish your posts.

Headlines grab attention

There's an art to writing good headlines for your posts; a boring headline could mean nobody reads your excellent content which you spent 2 hours writing. Make your readers want to read your post right away. It takes practice and a little confidence to come up with good headlines.

Here are some examples of good headlines:

- "The secret to living past 100"
- "7 worst mistakes people make when choosing runners"
- "How to check your own posture"
- "Little known way to make your office chair comfortable"

- "Get rid of back pain once and for all"
- "14 little things you can do to improve your metabolism"
- "Social anxiety: is it real or is it in your head?"

A quick search will reveal many guidelines on the Internet for writing headlines. Also refer to the section on Search Engine Optimisation, later in this book, since headlines and titles play a major part in how well pages rank in search results.

Guest blog posts

You don't need to personally write every post. You can get guest bloggers or your staff to add posts with their own unique style and take on things. However, you need to ensure that it all fits well with your content strategy. Ensure that the author is identified clearly along with any credentials and background. You may also like to offer a link back to the author's website or own blog.

Leverage your blog for sales

Referring back to the section on lead conversion earlier in this book, your ultimate goal in all this is to improve your business. Your practice blog has the potential to become one of the most valuable piece of sales material you have. Naturally incorporating your services and calls-to-action in your post is an excellent way to add a sales spiel without reducing the value offering of your content.

Don't tell readers how awesome your practice is; let your content speak for itself and readers will decide this for themselves.

Connect with readers

Encourage feedback, discussions and interactivity by asking your readers a question at the end of your post. Respect readers; respond to all comments.

It happens – you get the odd negative comment or rant from a reader. Removing comments or ignoring them often leads to more negative comments. Behave appropriately, focus on turning the negative experience into a positive one.

Promoting your blog

Even great content can go unnoticed. When you've written an excellent post, don't be shy – let the world know. Introduce it in your next newsletter. Send out an email to your colleagues and referrers inviting them to take a look. Share links to your posts on your social media channels (e.g. Facebook page). Encourage social media followers and readers of your blog post to share it further, to their friends.

Cross-linking to other posts in your blog encourages readers to spend more time exploring. Linking to other websites of authority is like using citations in a book – it adds credibility to your post. In some cases it can also help you get links back. Offer to be a guest writer or contributor to other blogs as appropriate, and ask for a link back.

Optimising your posts for search engines in mind will help them be found easily. It'll also help raise your website's overall profile in search engines. However, remember that your post should be primarily written to give value to your readers, not search engines.

"RSS feeds" enable readers to "follow your blog" and get notified when you add a new post. Ensure that RSS feeds are enabled with your blog, so that people can follow it easily. Talk with your web developer about this.

A simple and obvious tip to promote your blog is to include a link to it in your email signature. Every time you send an email, you're advertising your blog.

Google Authorship

Google Authorship allows linking between your personal profile with the content you author online. There are many benefits to this, including getting more attention when your blog posts are listed in search results. This is covered later in this book.

Follow other blogs

Find and follow other blogs of interest. Get involved and leave (positive) comments when you find something interesting. Getting involved is a great way to get noticed, get informed and get followers yourself.

Don't quit

Remember once again – it takes time and practice. It may take weeks or months to get into a routine. Plan ahead for your writing and post in advance (schedule) to make your job easier.

Online video

There's something special about video. It can communicate so much in such a compact package. We've discussed that the average person's attention span is getting shorter and shorter online. With all the information that's available, people are becoming more selective. However, think about the last time you landed on a web page with a title of interest and loads of text. You're happy to skim down the page, but hesitant to read it all, before you notice the video frame with the circle and triangle in it – universal icon for "play". Wouldn't you click it?

Video didn't just become popular recently. It would ALWAYS have been popular, had today's Internet speeds, access to good equipment and simplified software been around. According to some sources, approximately 90% of information transmitted to the brain is visual, and visuals are processed 60,000 times faster in the brain than text[3].

Today, more than 50% of Internet traffic is video data[4] and 70 hours of video is uploaded online every minute. More than 1 billion users visit YouTube each month, spending more than 4 billion hours watching videos[5].

76% of marketers plan to add video to their sites, making it a higher priority than Facebook, Twitter and blog integration[6]. 90% of shoppers found video helpful when making buying decisions online. Users are 64% more likely to make a purchase or enquiry if a website has video[7]. Viewers retain 95% of a message when they watch it in a video compared to 10% when reading it in text. 80% of users recall a video ad they viewed in the past 30 days[8].

---

[3] 3M Corporation & Zabisco

[4] Cisco

[5] YouTube

[6] Social Media Examiner

[7] comScore

[8] Online Publishers Association

Video in email marketing campaigns increased click-through-rates by 96%[9] and revenue by 40%[10]. Emails with explainer videos increased click-through-rates by 100% to 300%[11].

Video also has benefits for your website's search engine rankings. YouTube (owned by Google) is the world's second biggest search engine and accounts for 28% for all searches online. Having relevant videos in YouTube also means they can be shown in "blended" search results in a regular Google search. These have a much higher click through rate than regular search results. The chance of a page one listing on Google increases by 53 times with a video[12].

Why do video?

We've covered some interesting stats, but what does it all mean? Why is video so popular?

Video is easy to consume, it's great for conveying information and intent in a compact form. It's personal, it's appreciated. It puts a face to your business. It builds trust and familiarity for you as an individual and your practice. It's an extension of who you are. Video has the power to connect emotionally, personally. Therefore, it engages and connects better than other mediums. It allows deeper connection.

---

[9] Implix
[10] Relevancy Group
[11] Implix & Forrester Research
[12] Forrester Research

> When given the option between text and video, people will
> regularly choose video. It works for people with limited attention
> span. It's shareable.

People love video, and so do search engines. The technology available to everyone today means that there has never been a better time use video for your practice.

A young migrant in the US, Gary Vaynerchuk, grew his family wine store from $4 million in sales to over $60 million in sales in 5 years through his regular video blog, the Wine Library TV. He didn't want to write, but he sure could stand in front of a camera to share his knowledge and passion for wine with the world. With his amateur looking videos, he positioned himself as a non-snob expert who appealed to the average wine drinker with his style.

Alex Ikonn and his wife Mimi created "Luxy Hair", selling hair extensions. Their primary marketing is done via their YouTube channel comprised almost exclusively of how-to style videos. They have built a follower base of 1.7 million viewers and nearly 200 million total video views in little more than 4 years. Now they have a seven-figures-a-year business by providing useful, interesting and sought-after content with a genuine intent to help viewers, not a sales pitch. The interesting thing here is that they don't even feature their hair extension products in most of their videos.

For use by small business, video is still relatively unique, new and interesting. In your practice, it will help you build rapport, authenticity, trust and familiarity quickly since it conveys your passion, sincerity and amicability. These are very important, since your business is all about health services to people – you need all the help you can get in reducing resistance and ignorance while standing out from the crowd and building your business.

Video for local private practice

Your business involves working closely with people; there is inherent trust and rapport. This is why staff photos are important on your website. Similarly, you can leverage video to communicate as a real person with your audience at a deeper level than just text.

Videos help you become the face of your business.

A home page video is a great way to establish who you are and what you do. The average user's visit to a standard (text-image based) website lasts less than 1 minute. For a web page with video, the average visit lasts more than 5 minutes. A website's conversion rates (i.e. people taking a desired action) also increase where a relevant video is present.

Finally, it's surprisingly cheap and easy to produce good, valuable and sought after content. So why aren't you doing it?

Why you're not doing video

If you are not yet convinced, chances are you think that you need to be producing some kind of professional, polished production worthy of primetime TV, or the next viral video that gets millions of views in 2 months. You don't need big-budgets, concepts, storyboards, casting or pre-production. What you want is a means of quickly and easily connecting with your audience, putting a face to your practice and getting prolific with content creation.

You will probably also feel a little (or very much) intimidated being in front of a camera.

The fact is that people appreciate and expect videos produced by local businesses to be a little rough around the edges. It shows authenticity. As long as you let your personality and passion merge with valuable content, you'll get and hold attention. You can do this right now, with equipment you probably already have.

Get comfortable and confident in front of the camera. Choose a low-risk topic to get started. You'll probably think that your first few videos are embarrassing; that's fine. Aim to offer value and get it out there nevertheless. Practice makes perfect.

Don't be disheartened if you see no results after creating and putting up a few videos. It takes time, patience and practice plus experience to know what your audience wants.

Types of video to produce

Here are some ideas for videos you can produce for your practice.

- Walking tour of your practice and your facilities. You can also introduce staff. Ideal for your homepage.
- What you do: overview of your services and the benefits you offer.
- Presentation to camera, where you state your message direct to the audience, looking into the camera. You could speak about specific treatments or conditions or answer FAQs. You could demonstrate use of equipment or techniques.
- Invite people to ask questions on your website, and answer them on camera. Q&A sessions are great for

connecting with clients and building a solid YouTube channel.

- Interviews of other professionals and thought leaders.
- Get interviewed yourself, speaking to someone who is off-camera. This helps if you feel uncomfortable talking to the camera directly.
- Video blogs: you don't need to limit yourself to typing out your blog posts. Video may be easier, quicker or better suited to your style.
- Testimonials and case studies (as appropriate). These are very powerful marketing tools.
- Training videos: anything from classes to new employee instruction.
- Waiting room / reception videos, for looping mode display on a flat screen monitor or TV.
- Videos linked to email campaigns. An email that contains a screenshot of your video with a "play" button will receive more responses.
- Videos for specific patients. You can set a video as "private", so that only the intended viewers can access them.

Not all videos need to be done in front of camera. Another common format is using special software to record your computer screen while you present a slideshow and talk into a microphone. This way you don't need to appear in the video at all.

Getting started can be daunting. You can wet your feet with simpler, "low-risk" videos, such as:

- Frequently Asked Questions.
- Questions that clients should be asking.

- Educate new clients: What to expect when they get there for their first appointment. What is the intake process? Do they need to prepare in some way?
- Demonstrate common techniques or exercises.
- Highlights from an event. These work great with music overlay.

Consider the type of videos that you could do regularly. Remember that regular, consistent content is very important in building an audience.

Planning ahead

The equipment like cameras, microphones and lighting are all important. But most important is the message you want to convey. Don't go and get yourself a fancy new camera yet. Fancy graphics and equipment won't make up for bad content.

Topic

What is your goal with your video? To educate, engage or promote? Do you plan on repurposing your videos later (e.g. as course material or a podcast)?

Consider your topic for each video. To get started, you can build on content you've already created, such as a blog post that received lots of interest. Well-defined, focussed topics are easier than abstract topics that need exploration and detailed forethought. Start out picking the low-hanging fruit to gain experience and momentum.

Make content, not ads.

Brainstorm topics based on what you know and what your audience will love. As discussed earlier, you can keep a list of topic ideas from which to produce videos. This will also help you save time later, by rearranging and batch-producing some related topic videos together in the one hit.

Audience

As with any other type of content, consider your audience and their level of knowledge on your topic. Consider their needs – what do they want to see? Are they there for some instruction and education? What value are you providing with your video content?

Structure

Have a solid beginning (intro, welcome message), middle (meat in the sandwich), and a strong finish. Make the viewer feel like their time was well spent. People decide whether they will keep watching or not in the first 15 seconds of your video.

Message

Your message, knowledge and passion in your video is much more important than its production quality. What do you want your audience to take away from your video? You're close to your subject matter, so it may be difficult for you to see your message from the point of view of your audience.

> Get the attention of your audience by exciting them from the start. Introduce your topic and what you'll cover. Tell an interesting story where appropriate. People love stories and anecdotes.

What's your clear message? Stick to 1 or 2 key points. It's easier to remember these points and talk freely in your video than to memorise an entire script or read from notes. Think about the time when you talked to a friend about your holiday or when a friend asked you for a restaurant recommendation. Did you have a script written?

You've spent a lot of energy and resources to make a video. If the viewer has sat through to the end of your video, then it was obviously of value to them. Let them know what to do next. It could be to subscribe to your newsletter or YouTube channel, leave comments, thumbs-up the video, watch a related video, check out your website or call your reception for an appointment.

Duration

Short and sweet; this is the rule of thumb. 1-2 minute videos generally get more views than long videos, unless you're providing detailed educational course material. Each minute is about 150 words. If you're demonstrating something visually, keep it simple and clear. Make multiple videos if necessary.

Things you'll need

Once you have planned your message and scripted it, the shooting and production of the video is relatively straightforward.

Don't be overly eager and go out to buy an expensive camera. Much of the results you need can be achieved with relatively inexpensive equipment. You can always hire specialist equipment later on, before the need to purchase arises.

Just like equipment, you don't need professional operators either. You can pretty much do almost everything you need by yourself or with a little help.

Camera

At the risk of being shot down by professional video producers, I will tell you that most smartphones today will shoot pretty good (if not excellent) video that'll be perfect for your needs.

The advantages of using a smartphone are that you probably already have one and they're rather easy to use for video, compared to more professional equipment. They're less intrusive than other cameras and can even help with editing and uploading right from within the device.

Well, what are the disadvantages of using smartphones for video? The built in apps may not offer enough flexibility once you're proficient at using them. Their microphones are generally suited for phone calls instead of sounds generated a few metres away. Also the video can be very shaky, since the device itself is very light.

Here are some of today's best smartphones, when it comes to video.

- Apple iPhone 5, Apple iPhone 5C, Apple iPhone 5S
- HTC One
- Sony Xperia Z1
- Nokia Lumia 1020
- LG G2
- Samsung Galaxy S4, Samsung Galaxy S4 Zoom

Remember that this list will change rapidly. Simply search in Google for an updated list and compare devices if you're in the market for a new one.

What to look out for in a smartphone for video:

* High Definition (HD) video shooting
* Microphone jack
* Lots of storage (32GB+)
* Good size, high resolution screen

When using a smartphone, ensure that you're using the rear-facing camera. You may be tempted to use the front camera so that you can see yourself, but the front camera is usually lower quality and generally shoots in the 4:3 format instead of the 16:9 wide-screen format.

Another common mistake when shooting vide on your smartphone is to hold the phone upright. Remember to hold the phone on its side, so that you shoot in landscape mode.

As far as general quality goes, consumer handy-cams are better alternatives than the smartphone camera (if you already have one or can spare extra cash). Again, look for HD recording and external microphone jack.

DSLR cameras are the larger, more professional photo cameras. Some of these can shoot video extremely well. They are bulkier and more expensive. With interchangeable lenses and loads of attachments, you can get some really good video and special effects using a DSLR camera. However, they require lots of experience and skill to get maximum benefit. Not recommended for the average practice owner unless you want to explore photography and video in depth.

Storage media

Recording video requires a lot of storage on your camera. If you're using a smartphone, it'll have built in memory for storage. Some smartphones allow upgrading of their storage and some may be fixed. As a guide, aim to have about 32GB storage or more on your device.

If using camcorders and DSLR cameras, remember that they don't typically come with storage – you need to purchase it. Using SD cards for data storage is useful especially if your computer has a card-reader for easy transfer of files. Speak with a salesperson for a suitable memory card, since some will be too slow to write video data.

In any case, you will need to regularly move your video files off your device (or SD memory card) to your computer, so that you can clear up the storage space for more video recording. If using a smartphone, you may find that deleting some apps or other data will clear up some storage space for you.

Sound

Bad sound stands out like a sore thumb. Audiences will forgive bad video, but not bad sound. Imagine watching a video where the image freezes occasionally, but sound is not interrupted. You would forgive this more than if the audio kept freezing instead.

> Viewers are more willing to forgive bad video, but not bad audio.

Whether you're using a smartphone, camcorder or DSLR, you should ensure that your device has an external microphone jack. Plugging in an external microphone means that you can get closer to the sound source, so you can be heard more clearly. With smartphones, the headphone jack also serves as a microphone jack.

There are many types of microphones available. To start with, I'd recommend a lapel microphone, which is typically attached to the speaker's collar. Shotgun microphones are excellent, but possibly an overkill for your needs. For smartphones, sometimes you can get away with using the supplied headset (which also has a built-in microphone). You could simply paperclip it to your collar with the microphone hole facing out.

The importance of having a quiet environment goes without saying. Air conditioners, peak-hour traffic, barking dogs and people's chatter will be distracting. If you're in a room with little furniture or wooden floorboards, you may also experience the "closed room echo". Choose your location wisely and do some test runs before shooting.

Tripod

In most cases, you'll have a fixed camera location where the camera stays put from the start of the recording through to the end. Having someone hold the camera is fine, but holding the camera steady isn't as easy as you'd think. Having a tripod to fix your camera on means you can avoid shaky and wobbly video. It also means you won't need help from someone else.

You can get a basic tripod for about $50. There are also "table-top" tripods available. These are fine, but not as versatile. Most cameras will have tripod mounts, which attach the camera to the tripod securely. If you're using a smartphone, you can buy tripod-phone adaptors for a few bucks from EBay, where the phone sits snugly in the adaptor that attaches to the tripod.

When using a tripod to record yourself, you need to be able to start and stop the recording. Some cameras will have remote controls to do this. Most smartphones can do this using the buttons on the headset (which is useful if using it as a microphone as described earlier). Otherwise, it's perfectly fine to stand up and walk to the camera to start or stop recording. These bits can be easily edited out of the video later.

If you need a moving shot, you'll obviously want someone to hold the camera. Moving shots are required for things like tours of your practice, introducing staff while they work or demonstrating equipment or techniques. Moving shots can be tricky for the person with the camera. Just remember to keep camera movements slow and smooth, while keeping the subject in the frame and in focus. It may help to lean against a wall, to help steady the camera more. It takes practice.

Location

Choose a place that is well lit (natural lighting preferred), quiet and without many visual distractions. The location tells a story; if you're treating a patient in your video, you need to shoot the video in your treatment room. Your location gives a window into your world.

The background is of particular importance. Where is the subject in relation to the background? What colours are there? What objects are there? Are there distractions? Will you be sitting or standing?

> Give some thought to framing the background and your subject within the background.

If seated, avoid fidgeting and noise by using a chair that won't swivel. Avoid being up against a wall that will cast distracting shadows. Be the most interesting thing in the frame – dress and present yourself well.

If walking around during your shoot, make sure the pathway is tidy and well-lit all the way. If you're shooting on location (outside of your clinic), avoid windy areas that can cause unwanted microphone noise. Cloudy days work better than sunny days for improved lighting. Beware of your surroundings.

Lighting

Photography and video rely on light. Good lighting is crucial for good video. It may be confusing at first when you realise that your camera doesn't see things in the same way as your eyes do. This is why you see too many dark scenes, too much yellow or blue in amateur videos.

Use natural light (daylight) whenever possible. Artificial lights (bulbs, halogen, fluorescent etc.) are fine, but you need to deal with them specifically. Many cameras try to detect and handle artificial light, but when this fails, you end up with a video that looks too yellow or blue.

Try to have more than one light source to avoid unwanted shadows (especially on the face). Lighting up your subject from 3 points is ideal. 3-point lighting is where you have one light shining on the subject's face from one side, a softer fill-in light from the other side plus one light shining on the background to brighten it up and remove any shadows. Here it what 3-point lighting looks like:

3 point lighting:

If your lights are harsh, they'll cast sharp shadows. Diffusing the light with tracing paper or baking paper will make the light softer and create nicer shadows.

There are countless videos and tutorials on YouTube for all this.

Teleprompters

A teleprompter is a piece of equipment that newsreaders and other professionals use to read a script while still looking straight into a camera. They can be expensive and tricky to use. Unless you'll be doing long videos and need to read a script while looking into the camera, you're better off practicing a few times and winging it.

Chances are that for most videos you'll be doing, you already know your subject matter so well that you can talk to a friend about it for a few minutes without reading something. Pretend you're talking to a friend rather than the camera and avoid reading stuff. It's more authentic and personable.

Software

Once you have your video footage, you need a means of editing it to get the best bits into one finished video. For this, you'll need some basic software on your computer, such as

- Microsoft Movie Maker on PC
- iMovie on Mac
- Camtasia on Mac (capable of recording your computer screen too; good for presentations and recorded webinars)

There are many free or cheap desktop computer software available. More on these later, in post-production. You could even use apps on your smartphone (iMovie or Reel Director on iOS, Magisto and VidTrim on Android) to edit and upload your videos, but this could get fiddly.

Action!

Preparing yourself

Getting in front of the camera to present something for the first time can be daunting. Remember one thing: it's not a live broadcast. You can re-shoot as many times as you want. Take your time and practice. Get comfortable. Your audience is interested in your knowledge, experience, tips and insights.

Unless you're preparing a long video with detailed content, you shouldn't really need cue cards or teleprompter scripts. Just remember the key points in your message and your intent behind each video. Being yourself, letting your passion, energy and personality come through is the best thing you can do.

Wear suitable attire, avoiding thin stripes and colours that blend into your background. Colour accents are great. Make sure that you fill the frame nicely. Don't stand too far, unless you are demonstrating techniques or have other people in the shot. If you're solo, make sure the focus is on you.

Practice looking straight into the camera – imagine that you're talking to a person and the camera is where their eyes would be. This can be very tricky at the start. If it helps, you can get someone to stand behind the camera and fix your eyes on him or her.

Recording

OK, it's finally time to shoot.

Ensure that you have enough data storage and battery juice on your camera. Do some test recordings and make notes about your setup, so it is easier next time.

If you're shooting by yourself, make sure you do a few test runs and check to see that you're framed nicely within the background. Use of a tripod is essential. You should move the tripod as required, until you find the best position. Also check the sound quality. You may need to plug in a headset to your camera to hear it clearly.

> It is fine to get up and down from your seat to press the start/stop button – these frames can be edited out later.

Make sure you get all footage you'll need before going to your computer for editing. If you missed something, it's harder to go back to your setup and do more recording. It's fine to do multiple takes; you only need one good shoot and you can discard the rest.

Check that you actually recorded each take. It's quite easy to miss the record button and give a presentation, only to realise that you weren't even recording!

Post-production

Transferring footage to computer

Each time you press start and stop, a file is saved to your camera's data storage. These files need to be transferred to your computer before you can edit and upload to the Internet.

With all the test shots and outtakes, it's easy to build up hundreds or even thousands of videos quickly.

Make a habit of creating a new folder for each day (or topic) you shoot. Name the folders clearly so you can find them later.

How you transfer your files from your camera to your computer will vary depending on your camera and computer. Most often, attaching your camera or SD card to your computer will enable you to open the contents in a file explorer. You can move them as regular files. Just do a search on YouTube and you will find dozens of instructional videos to help you.

After you have copied your files to your computer, verify that you have actually done so. Disconnect your camera (or your SD card) from your computer and play each video file you just shot. The last thing you want is to delete the videos from your camera and realise that you hadn't copied them over correctly.

Videos can take up lots of storage space. After you have your files safely on your computer, you can delete the videos from your camera. This will make more space on your storage card for more videos later.

Similarly, you can delete the videos you will never need from your computer. These are the test shots you did and any obvious outtakes. Leaving only the useful video snippets will make your job easier when it comes to editing.

Editing

Editing is where you clean up, trim, adjust, cut and paste your videos together. Your video may have bad lighting or audio. It may need some trimming at the start or at the end. Maybe you have several videos that you need to join together into one. The aim of editing is to end up with a finished, polished video.

Sometimes, your video may be good enough without editing. If it's a short video that starts and ends well in one single shoot, you may be happy to leave it as it is. You can even upload it straight to your YouTube account from your smartphone.

Video editing requires some software to be installed on your computer. Professional video editing software can set you back thousands of dollars and 2 years in learning to use it. Luckily, there is some very good software available for the amateur user that will do pretty much everything you'll want to do on your own. Remember, the goal is not to become a filmmaker.

If you're on a PC, your computer may already have the software "Windows Movie Maker" installed. If not, you can download and install it for free. Your best bet on a Mac is iMovie, which is preinstalled on all new Macs (and can be downloaded for older Macs).

I originally considered including instructions for using these software in this book. However, there are plenty of very good instructional videos available on using these software. Simply search on YouTube for something like "windows movie maker for beginners" or "iMovie for beginners". You'll find dozens of very good step-by-step videos to teach you video editing. Remember that there are different versions of various software, so search for videos that match the software and version you are using.

Note that your smartphone may also have some video editing apps available. However, you may find these difficult to use on a regular basis, due to the limited screen real estate available. Editing video on a desktop computer is much easier.

Make sure you have all the video footage you need before you start editing. It doesn't matter if you shot them out of sequence – you can edit them back into correct sequence easily. It's like sorting event photos into a logical story-telling order, even if they were taken out of sequence.

Here are some edits you will probably want to make:

- Trim the start and ends so that you delete any "Are we rolling? Shall I start?" moments.
- Fix lighting issues (make overall video brighter or darker).
- Fix colour issues (if your video is too blue or too yellow).
- Stitch several videos together or reorder them.
- Add transition effects (e.g. cross-fade from one shot to the next).

- Use template videos for a consistent start and end message across all your videos (e.g. add the same call-to-action message to several videos).
- Add text headings or captions to your video.
- Add a music soundtrack.

You can also do some basic editing directly after you upload your video to YouTube, such as lighting and colour correction and replacing the audio with music. However, you'll probably find it quite limited.

Special effects

You know how annoying it is if you've ever seen a slideshow presentation where someone has gone crazy with special effects and transitions. It's the same with video. Most video editing software has an assortment of available special effects and transitions. It's best to stick to the basics, such as fade through from one scene to the next.

Avoid spinning, whirling and other distracting effects – they're too "trying too hard" and passé.

Soundtrack

Adding a musical background to your video can truly enhance it. However, this is something that takes considerable thought. You want to ensure that it's suited and supports your message rather than distracting from it. Also you need to check for any possible copyright infringements. Chances are you will need to purchase a commercial licence to use music in your video.

YouTube has a range of royalty-free music available for you to use, if you like. You can use YouTube's built-in editing features to add them to your video, after uploading it to YouTube.

Exporting and uploading

There are many places where you can upload your video. You can even upload straight to your website, like you would upload any photo.

However, the recommended platform is YouTube. It's owned by Google and is the second largest search engine in the world. With so many viewers daily, your videos have the best chance for exposure when uploaded to YouTube.

If you have a Google account, you can already login to YouTube and start uploading. The best thing to do, though, is to create a "channel" for your practice. You would then upload all your practice-related videos to your channel, where they would all be grouped together. This is covered in more detail later in this book.

If you have a quick video on your smartphone that already looks good in its raw state, you can upload to your YouTube channel straight from your phone. If your video is on your desktop computer, you'll need to "export" it as a single finished file before uploading to YouTube. Most video editing software will facilitate uploading a video straight to YouTube. Otherwise, you can manually upload a video file to YouTube. YouTube supports the following file formats:

- MPEG4
- 3GPP
- MOV

- WebM
- MPEGPS
- WMV
- FLV

Preferred resolution for export should be 16:9 aspect ratio at 1280×720 pixels.

> Uploading a video may take a long time. Plus, YouTube may take its time processing the video before it's available for the public. Be patient.

Once uploaded and processed by YouTube, you will need to specify various settings, title and descriptions for your video. These are covered later in the book.

Sharing your videos

Once your video makes YouTube its home, it's ready for people to view it. You can grab some "embed code" for your video to insert it into a page on your website. For example, you can embed a video to your home page – where the video itself lives in YouTube, but it can be played directly from your home page. This is great, since embedding is easy and you don't need to worry about uploading to your website or bandwidth limitations on your server.

If you need, you can mark a video as "private" in YouTube, which means that it will not show up in search results – the only way to view that video is by giving someone a direct URL link. This is a good feature if you plan on producing private, one-on-one videos for specific clients.

You can easily share your videos from your YouTube channel on your Facebook page. Facebook also allows you to upload videos straight to your Facebook page (instead of uploading to YouTube first). In either case, you want your video to be uploaded to your YouTube channel at least.

Maximum value

Whether your videos took minutes to shoot and upload or hours of preparation and production, you'll want to extract maximum value from them online. Your key driver is to offer value to your viewers and reach as far and wide as possible. The work has been done, and it's now time to leverage it.

The best online videos are those that are shared. A key metric for measuring the performance of online video is the number of times the video has been shared. Keep them short, interesting and valuable for the most sharing potential.

With your videos, you can:

- Build a regular video blog.
- Add on regular calls-to-action after each video.
- Have it transcribed into a blog post (excellent idea for SEO and viewers who may want to print it out).
- Embed your videos on your website pages.
- Extract MP3 audio (great for uploading as a podcast, so people can listen on the run).
- Add clickable links through to your website, social media profiles, email newsletter signup forms, enquiry pages or appointment pages or other related content (YouTube makes this easy).

- Encourage comments from visitors and develop discussions within your YouTube channel.

- Add a video link (with a thumbnail image) to your email signature or your newsletter.

All this from one sitting of a video recording. Talk about getting prolific!

Book-ending your videos

"Book-ending" is when you start your videos with a common intro and outro. For example, your intro may be some fancy animation or logo while you deliver a common, consistent spiel. Your outro could show your contact details, website and practice address, with a call-to-action. Your call-to-action should include a reminder to subscribe to your channel, reminder to like/add to favourites/share your video and leave comments.

Using the same "book-ends" in each video creates consistency, familiarity, trust and branding. It also adds plenty of production value.

The good thing is that you probably need to generate only one set of intro/outro pairs. You can then tack this onto every video you create using your editing software.

> You can have these made for you very cheaply – search for "video intro" at **fiverr.com**.

Content syndication

You don't need to stop with just YouTube. You can create accounts and channels with many other video hosting services around, such as vimeo.com. There are services that assist you in creating and managing your video hosting accounts and distributing your videos to multiple targets at once, so you don't need to do this manually every time.

Video tips

Video gets easier with practice. Here are some tips you can use to make it more effective, efficient or fun.

- Start with easy topics such as explaining particular conditions you treat or techniques you perform. You can build on existing content, like supplementing an information article on your website with a video demonstration.

- Focus on one key message per video. Your viewer has clicked "play" to get questions answered. Ensure you answer the question.

- You're human – don't be robotic and deliver a monotonous speech from a written script. Relax and smile. Remember; you know your topic already. Just deliver it like you would any other day. Show your passion.

- It may help to have someone sit next to the camera – look at them (as if you are being interviewed) instead of the camera. Looking at the camera is not always easy.

- Practice a couple of times beforehand if you need.

- Look presentable. Reduce visual and noise distractions from the scene. Eliminate any behavioural distractions – people tend to fidget unwittingly.

- Feel free to be entertaining and let your personality show through.

- It's fine to be informal, but stick to the topic; don't ramble on unnecessarily. Keep it short and sweet.
- Have a strong finish, with a clear call-to-action. Thank your audience for watching.
- If using a smartphone, switch on "flight-mode" to avoid interruptions during recording.
- Watch and review yourself (what is your audience going to be seeing?) Re-record if necessary. You likely won't get it right at first go.

Getting professionals

DIY video is completely acceptable and you can get some great results these days. Especially for the shorter, regular content pieces you need to produce.

However, if you want a more professional-grade video (longer than a couple of minutes) to introduce your practice, you may want to hire professionals.

Entry-level videos by professionals start at about $1,000. This typically includes an hour or two of preparation and recording, plus some editing. Decent quality productions range up to $5,000 for better storyboarding, finish quality, equipment and editing. It's unlikely that you'll need anything more than this. Corporate-grade quality productions for your practice can cost upwards of $20,000. Unnecessary overkill.

Other content offerings

EBooks

Articles and blog posts on your website are typically a few hundred words. EBooks on the other hand are more comprehensive and cover a topic (or a group of topics) in detail. An eBook can be 10-30 pages (2500-7500 words) or more. Think of it like a chapter of a book.

> EBooks are intended to be distributed in electronic format (typically PDF files), which can be downloaded (and printed if required).

Just like regular books, eBooks need extensive thought, research and editing, since this is the expectation from the reader. It'll be worthwhile getting a designer for layout, presentation and illustrations. Cover design will be a major consideration. It could turn out to be a lot of work, but it's something you can leverage for years.

As always, the content must be valuable! People must want it and ask for it. It must be something that people will be willing to pay for, even though you won't necessarily charge for it. Think of topics that can be covered in detail and appeal to many people.

Although you can sell an eBook, you can gain more from leveraging it to collect email addresses for your mailing list (covered in the next chapter). People will be willing to give you their email address in return for downloading your eBook. Thus your eBook becomes a lead magnet as well as positioning you as an expert.

Information sheets

These are one or two page handouts that your clients can collect from your reception. They can cover common topics related to your service.

If you have good content on your website, you can get away with simply printing them and stacking them up on a brochure stand at your front desk.

To make these more professional, you can get a designer to prepare a design template complete with your logo and contact details. Simply change the title and content as you need.

> You can also save these as PDF files, so that your website visitors can download them.

Screencasts, webinars and podcasts

A screencast is a video recording of your computer screen. It can be used to great effect when presenting a slideshow while you talk. Because it's recorded, viewers can access your presentation at any time.

A webinar is like a seminar that is delivered online, where you are the presenter and the attendees are listening to you while viewing your slideshow from your computer. Essentially, it's a live screencast. Webinars also allow the audience to ask questions in real-time, while you're presenting.

Podcasts are video or sound-only recordings. They are formatted for consumption on mobile devices on the go. Many people have created channels where audiences tune in to download regular content.

Screencasts, webinars and podcasts are more advanced topics for online content. They can be very beneficial for your practice and are worth considering.

Your publishing rhythm

There is no doubt, as many benefits as it offers to your practice, publishing content is hard work – especially in the beginning. Here's a rough guide for planning your schedule. Just like keeping a list of topic ideas on your computer will help you with what to write, keeping a calendar will help you plan out when to write.

Website pages: There are only so many topics you can cover about the services you offer, symptoms you treat or techniques you use in your practice. Once you've built a good library, you can focus on other types of content. It's a good idea to have most of these pages done when your website launches. However, you should revisit and update periodically.

Blog posts: Aim to do one post per week. Note that you can schedule post to "go live" at a certain date, so you can write and upload in bulk.

Videos: You'll create some videos as one-offs (introduction, practice tour etc.), whereas there will be other videos you produce as a part of a series (Q&A sessions, demonstrations, video blogs etc.). Aim for 1-2 videos a month. If you're doing a video blog, aim for one video per week.

EBooks & information sheets: Aim for one of these every 1-2 months.

Screencasts, webinars and podcasts: These are more likely to be produced on an "as needed" basis. However, they'll make good additions to your YouTube channel, along with your other videos.

Profile: Getting the word out

Marketing your website is not about hits or visits, but people. There is no magic bullet – different things work for different businesses. The key is to test, measure and then determine what works for you.

Since starting his online business,
Carl stopped getting out of his pyjamas in the morning.

Marketing your website isn't just about getting more traffic – it's about getting more targeted traffic, i.e. people who could potentially become your clients or become involved with your business in some other way. It's no use getting 2000 visitors to your website a month, if none are interested in what you offer.

The second objective of marketing for your website is to convert these prospects – i.e. to take some action, whether that's to book an appointment, call you up or get involved in some way.

Some ingredients of online marketing (regardless of your tools) are:

- Increasing your authority and becoming a valuable resource.
- Increasing your online visibility.
- Improving your standing with search engines.
- Establishing yourself or your business in social media.
- Knowing your advertisement options and running ad campaigns.

You need to view marketing online (as with traditional marketing) as something you need to plan for and execute with regularity. Many practice owners achieve good results after some good marketing, but then they stop. This is a common mistake and results in the peaks and troughs prevalent in small business.

This chapter introduces you to a few key options when it comes to marketing online. Social media concepts are covered in the next chapter.

> Remember, it's easy to get overwhelmed with all the things you can do. So pick something that makes sense to you and give it time; tweak it, change your angle, test and measure.

These things take time so be consistent and don't just abandon something after only 2 weeks.

Outbound vs. inbound marketing

Today's consumers are empowered and will initiate most of the conversations that take place. Until recently, the goal of "marketing" was for a business to initiate such conversations. Today's savvy consumers are simply ignoring much of the ambient marketing chatter, with increasing efficiency.

Easy access to abundant information on just about everything under the sun has resulted in an overload for consumers; they now require more meaningful and useful communication with businesses, on their own terms. Hence, traditional marketing approaches are losing their effectiveness.

All marketing basically revolves around a funnel paradigm; marketers would fill the top of their sales funnel (generate leads and get attention) and then they would churn through the various stages of the funnel towards completing a sale or other desired outcome.

With the advent of online marketing and growing consumer awareness, the concepts of "outbound and inbound" marketing have emerged.

Outbound marketing is reliant on the traditional approaches:

- Letterbox drops
- Flyers
- Newspaper advertising
- Yellow Pages advertising
- Google AdWords / Facebook advertising
- Posters
- Letters
- Trade shows
- Cold calling

The problem with this type of marketing is that it's based largely on interrupting people and pushing something in their faces. Now that thousands of such messages a day are being thrown at them, consumers have become impatient with and desensitised against this form of marketing. Outbound marketing is also very expensive and difficult to measure in regard to returns; it's just "spray and pray".

People are figuring out creative ways to block them out (e.g. recording TV shows to fast forward ad breaks, caller IDs to block unwanted calls etc.) They're in better control of what they tune into and when.

Today the client calls the shots (and this is the way it should be). They're empowered, informed and connected. They have choices and they know it. And you know what? This is great for the small businesses that in the past have been ignored by clients because of bigger companies' marketing budgets.

"We need to stop interrupting what people are interested in and become what people are interested in."
~ Craig Davis, Chief Creative Officer, J. Walter Thompson

Although outbound marketing isn't completely ineffective, it's likely to reduce in effectiveness in the coming years.

Inbound marketing is different.

It doesn't go head to head with prospects that are trying to block you. Inbound marketing is where you set up your presence online (where clients are) and optimise it to get found by people who are already researching about or shopping for what you offer... Being in the right place at the right time.

Inbound relies on setting up your website to attract visitors naturally through search engines, blogs, articles, educational material and social media. It sets out knowing that people will accept social proof, testimonials and recommendations from trusted sources more than a random flyer in the letterbox. Inbound marketing aims to make you into such a trusted source.

Inbound marketing includes approaches such as:

- Having such great content on your website that search engines love to list your pages above other websites for similar searches.
- Being generous:
    - Website content
    - Blog posts

- eBooks
- Newsletters
- Articles
- White papers
- How-to videos
- Info graphics
- Online calculators
- Planning tools
- Podcasts
- Answers to common questions
- Anything that is share-worthy or has a value attached in the prospect's eyes

• Opt-in subscriptions (people sign up to your newsletter because you have something relevant and good to say).

• Social media presence (e.g. Facebook, YouTube, Google+).

• Not ignoring mobile device users.

• Becoming an authority in your field, a thought leader via your blog.

• Cultivating online communities.

• Conducting relevant and targeted communications rather than shotgun approaches.

It also requires systematic testing, measuring and tweaking your approaches to fine-tune them. When executed well, inbound strategies can make your marketing efforts more effective, leaner and more profitable for your practice.

It sounds like a lot of work, doesn't it? Well, the good news is that you can pick and choose your approach; you can start anywhere and see which ones resonate with you and get you the best results.

When done right, time spent communicating and establishing yourself in your industry will naturally lead to referrals, higher dollar value per transaction and more repeat visits in your practice.

Also, all this work will last much longer than any outbound marketing campaign. Valuable material you create will continue to market your practice even years into the future – in fact, it'll have a compounding effect with all the future inbound work you perform. Get comfortable in the new mediums – you'll need to spend lots of time there.

> Earn people's interest rather than buying it.

You may ask *what about word of mouth referrals?* Yes, WOM is great – it's almost a form of inbound marketing – however, it still largely relies on requesting a referral from your clients. A few will refer, most won't. It's not in your control.

There are still some benefits (and good results) to be had with outbound marketing methods – it's not dead yet. However, in preparation for the future and establishing momentum, you must consider making the transition to inbound marketing methods.

In my personal experience, I've found that a mix of outbound and inbound used together within a campaign can yield better results overall than either method used separately.

If your practice/business is relatively new, you'll probably rely more on outbound marketing initially, until you establish your presence. Though the results initially may be quicker, it'll cost more and it's not a good long-term strategy. During this time, you should not neglect inbound strategy development, for one day it may constitute your entire marketing strategy. Try to reach this point as soon as possible.

Your new marketing mix:

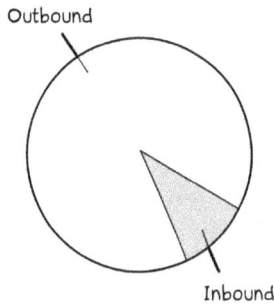

Marketers must work harder and smarter to keep pace with more sophisticated consumers. Inbound marketing is now the most effective way for marketers to generate real results.

Importance of regular contact

There is so much distraction available for the average person today – especially online. It's likely that someone will forget they visited a website or signed up for a newsletter very quickly. If a visitor has requested information from you or signed up to your newsletter, it shows that they're interested in what you're offering.

It's now up to you to ensure that interest is maintained. Remember that you need several "touches" with a subscriber before you build familiarity, and more so before they respond by taking action. Regular communication with your patients, prospects, subscribers and community is vital to build and maintain relationships. Remember, they're looking for direction or solutions.

In many cases, they'll need to be reminded of how you can solve their problems. They're likely to forget about your services, even with the genuine benefits they would receive from you. Regular communication in the form of emails, newsletters or even phone calls and postcards will ensure that this doesn't happen.

> Remember, the goal is to build a relationship – not get a new client directly.

So how regular is "regular"? Think 3-4 weeks. If you stretch your communications out to few months at a time, they'll surely forget you. Will they get tired of hearing from you? That depends on what value you provide – if you send the same update out each time, then they won't see the benefit in having their inbox filled with your emails. But if you offer timely, useful information and offers, they'll look forward to hearing from you. Furthermore, they'll expect it according to your regular schedule.

Search Engines

Search engines enable users of the World Wide Web to find information, such as dinner recipes, movie times, stock prices, rental apartments, used car parts, online accounting packages and of course, health related information among everything else.

There are 60 trillion individual pages on the web today and it's constantly growing. Search engines like Google seek out and index them, so that when someone searches for one of these pages, it could be listed in search results.

Of course, some search engines like Google and Bing are better at this than others. It's not enough just to be able to index as many pages as possible, though. When people use a search engine, they expect to find *relevant* search results.

If search results were consistently not useful, people would stop using that search engine. Hence, search engines are in the game of indexing AND returning relevant results to users.

Google is the most popular search engine in the world; it's the only one that really matters since it gathers over 70% of all search traffic. If your website is represented well with Google, chances are you'll do pretty well with the others.

Moving on to the bigger question: why would you want your website to rank high up in Google (i.e. have better representation)? Well, the answer is obvious, but here's a number: 90% of people won't bother scrolling down to the bottom of the results page and go to the second page when they search for something.

Most people who search using Google often find what they're looking for within the first page of results. If not, instead of going to the second page of results, they'll simply refine their search terms and try again.

Of course, there are exceptions. For example, if you were looking for something specific (let's say your accountant's website), then you would look beyond the first page.

So you want your practice website to list on the first page of Google's search results when someone searches for something you can help them with.

How search engines work

Search engines generally navigate from page to page by crawling. This means it scans a page while indexing its contents and finding links from that page to other pages to go to next.

During the indexing process, pages are sorted by their content and other factors such as general theme of a website and how each page of a website is linked to other pages on other websites. These are important metrics in determining how "popular" a website is, or how much authority it has. All this happens pretty much autonomously.

So you can imagine that this business of crawling can quickly get very complex as a search engine maps out the entire online landscape. Google's index is over 100 million gigabytes (if that means anything to you).

Your website's pages will be in there – somewhere.

What you (as the user) see is the second part of what search engines do. It sorts out this index to dig up search results whenever someone is looking for something, based on the "search terms" entered. There are programs and formulas (also known as algorithms) used to deliver the best results possible. When you search for something, the search engine looks for clues to better understand what you mean. The results are then ranked in order of what the search engine thinks you may be looking for. Google uses over 200 factors when ranking your results. These factors include things like

- A website's (or an individual page's) quality
- User context
- Freshness

- How established a website is

> In short, the search engine's goal is to deliver relevant results to the user.

For this reason, they often change the formula (algorithm) used to rank and display results. For example, the rise of social media means when ranking its website pages in search results, Google now considers what is being said about a business in social circles. This allows Google to remain a popular search engine.

As a side note, the differences in search results between Google and Bing for the same search term is due to the differences in their algorithms.

So if your website is not "ranking well" in Google (i.e. at the top of search results), it's because Google does not deem it to be relevant against the user's search criteria. We will explore what it takes to rank well as well as other options.

The search results page

Taking Google as our search engine of focus, the search results page consists of a few key elements:

Paid listings are frequently found across the top or side; somebody has paid money to Google to have these links appear on the search results page.

The main body of search results page are the "organic results" – i.e. not paid. Here you would find various types of listings, such as:

- **Regular listings**: i.e. a page from a website, with its title and description.

- **Map results**: commonly available when searching for something localised, such as a chiropractor, school or pizza restaurant.

- **Video results**: with thumbnails, so you can click and view the video.

Again, these are all based on relevance according to Google. It's common that the user doesn't find what they want immediately – so the search terms used can be tweaked to refine results or start a new search altogether.

Living to 100 years old

So, how do you get your website to the top of Google?

This is like asking, "How can I live to be 100 years old?" There's no one correct answer to this question, however, we know that there are many factors that influence one's likelihood of living to 100:

- General health
- Good habits
- Genetics
  etc.

Besides these generally accepted factors, there are a ton of other theories depending on whom you ask (like diet, happiness, circumstance and where you live). Noting that there are even cases of heavy smokers who live well into ripe old age, the answer to "how can I live to 100" becomes quite complex.

What complicates matters even more is when you consider "how you want to live"; do you want a full and happy life or simply survive to 100?

"How do I get my website to the top of search engines?" has no direct answer. It changes on a case-by-case basis. There are some basic factors that can be controlled (or designed) using proven guidelines to improve your chances, but the rest is generally a game of guesses, trial and error. A good SEO consultant on your side (like a personal trainer or a life coach) will be able to help you on your quest; just don't fall for the magic potion guys.

Where the analogy breaks down is that one person's accomplishment of hitting 100 does not hinder another person's chances. In search engines, however, there is an added element of scarcity – i.e. competition from other businesses that want the same top spots in search results.

Remember there are no guarantees, just like getting to 100 years old. There's only what you can do proactively to improve your chances and getting the right help to make it happen.

What factors determine a website's placement?

There are hundreds of factors that determine how well a website ranks for selected (target) keywords. These include:

- The content within your website (how relevant contents are to the search terms or keywords used by search engine users), and how well the information is organised and constructed.
- Quantity and quality of links to your website from other links (known as in-links).

- Quality and relevance of the websites providing you with these in-links.

- The age of your website and domain name.

- Amount of competition (number of websites) that want to rank well for the same search terms or keywords as you.

- Location of the business (also considers location of the search engine user).

- Individual personalisation preferences for each search engine user.

- Social mentions (e.g. you get mentioned in Twitter, Facebook etc.).

- Any blacklisting (a search engine may remove you altogether if it finds a breach of conduct).

- Many others.

What about public directories that point to your practice?

You may find that there are other websites that list your practice on a search engine. For example, you search for "Essendon Physiotherapy", and you find Yellow Pages or Google+ Local listing in the search results.

Listings like these are common. You may have specifically set these up (or even paid for them) or they may be auto-generated for you. In many cases, you are able to "claim" an auto generated listing and amend it.

It turns out that listings like these are not only very valuable on their own, but can also be interconnected in many ways. For example, having a properly claimed and configured Google+ Local page can help your website's ranking (or vice versa). Search engines are smart enough to know that these listings are for the same business.

This also touches on how search engines can link social activity to your website (e.g. someone tweeting something about your business, or sharing a page from your website on their Facebook wall). Again, they all work toward increasing the online authority of your practice and website.

Traditionally, SEO was all about what you can do within your website. Today, your website is still the mother ship and many external factors can influence how your website (or online presence) rank in search results.

Your website's authority is basically measured by how many people and other websites "talk" about your website. A link from one website to yours is like a vote; they're linking to you because their visitors would benefit from visiting your website. The weight of this vote depends on factors such as:

- Is the referring website of high authority itself?
- Is the referring website related in content to yours?
- In addition to a number of technical considerations.

Similarly, if lots of people are discussing your website in their social circles then it's safe for Google to assume that your website has authority.

> Your website authority plus relevance of your pages to the keywords used in the search generally determine how high your website is listed in search results.

Search Engine Optimisation (SEO) basics

First thing to say about SEO is that although it's important, it should never be your sole focus. There are many things you can do to make your website and content better. The essence of SEO, as far as search engines are concerned, is to give visitors what they want; so you should focus on that first and foremost.

As discussed, the trick with your website and content is then to make it relevant to your target prospects. Don't expect a badly prepared 3 page website with old content to rank well, unless you have absolutely no competition.

SEO is a very big topic. This is just an introduction so you can discuss it with confidence with a professional consultant. You can also get in touch with us at **practicepulse.com** for a copy of our SEO for local private practice eBook.

Creating meaningful, read-worthy content on your website is a great start for Google to start noticing your website and ranking it high on someone's search results.

For all intents and purposes, keywords, key phrases, search query and search terms all mean the same thing. It's what the search engine user enters into the search box – i.e. the thing they want to find online.

There are many aspects to SEO, and aligning your website with your "target keywords" is one of them.

Search engines determine the "authority" your website has on a given topic based on the content it finds on your website. Links from other websites to yours also build authority, since these are effectively "votes" for your website indicating that it has useful content.

The idea of SEO then is to make your website (or online presence) more attractive to search engines. Determining which keywords to target can be a challenge and an art in itself. There are several factors to consider, such as:

- What services you offer
- What services you want to promote
- What keywords are hard to target (because there are too many other websites that rank for those keywords)
- What keywords are more likely to convert when a visitor comes to your website
- What keywords are searched for most frequently that are also of interest to you

SEO strategies

Best SEO strategies revolve around techniques and tactics that focus on a human audience opposed to search engines and completely follows search engine rules and policies.

Here are some examples:

- Write or prepare quality content that people would search for (consider the keywords or search terms that people will use)

- Consider a good mix of media (e.g. videos, eBooks, articles, blog posts)
- Consider establishing good social media presence.
- Share your content abundantly, and encourage your visitors to share your content through their social circles too.
- Consider online listings that provide localised presence such as Google+ Local and Facebook Pages. These are important for local businesses such as your practice.
- Encourage discussions, comments, reviews, interaction and other activity online revolving around your online presence and website.
- Encouraging links to your website from other websites who share the same target audience (and linking to websites from yours as appropriate).

There are a number of technical requirements for good SEO, related to how your website is built. Your web developer should know about these and implement them.

Think of SEO as removing hurdles for search engines rather than getting search engines to rank your website higher.

Get started

Since one of the indicators of relevance is how established a website is, it's important to get started with and push your website with a solid strategy as early as possible. New websites take longer to start ranking well, especially if they're also using a new domain name. For example, all other things being the same, if the only thing difference between your competitor's website and yours is that they've been around longer, you'll struggle to compete unless you have much better (more relevant) content and apply other strategies.

SEO is one of the best long-term strategies (and investments) for generating website traffic.

On-page optimisation

On-page optimisation refers to the process of optimising specific sections of your site contents to make them clearer for users and search engines. This includes URLs, titles, headings, images, descriptions, links and of course content. The goal is to align any given page of your site closely with a specific topic. Generally, target keywords are pre-determined to identify what specific topic a page will be aligned with.

Your page titles and URLs are often the first thing indexed by search engines and can have a significant impact on how you are ranked.

Your URLs are the address of each page within your website, such as http://yourpracticename.com/services/our-top-service

These are generally created by your CMS. However, even by looking at it, you can generally tell what that page will be about. If it's cryptic and you can't tell what the page is about, then it's a bad URL structure; talk with your web developer to get it fixed.

Your page title is what appears as the blue link, in Google search results, for that page. Every page should have a title containing the most important words at the beginning of the title. Titles should be no more than about 70 characters. Most CMS packages will enable you to edit the title of each page in your website.

You may have heard about meta tags – these are bits of information built into the page, to describe the properties of that page to search engines. For example, in your Google search results page, you see a number of listings – the blue links are the titles, and the short introductory text under them is the description. This description was embedded into that page as a meta tag.

"Description meta" tags should be supplied for each page, and should be written carefully, not more than 155 characters. Most CMS packages will enable you to edit the description meta tag of each page in your website.

The "keywords meta tag" is pretty much ignored by search engines; there's little to no value in providing this meta tag information in a page.

Correct use of spelling and grammar are important in the eyes of Google. Make sure that you check over your contents before uploading.

Use of good internal links is recommended. You should provide suitable links from one page to another to make it easy for your visitors to reach relevant pages as required.

Use of valid HTML code is crucial. This is something your web developer will handle; you shouldn't need to worry about HTML. Sitemaps are something that your web developer would again need to handle. Though not necessary, sitemaps could help search engine crawlers find and index your website's pages.

Off-page optimisation

Let's consider two websites having similar content and age and targeting the same keywords. How could one rank much better than the other? One key driver is the website's reputation.

Google has a metric called "page rank" which is a measure of reputation and authority. Basically, the more external websites that link to yours, the more it's deemed popular (i.e. reputable). Links from one website to another is essentially a "vote", saying that website is a good resource.

So getting in-links to your website from external sources is important in building up your reputation (or page-rank). This concept was introduced earlier.

But not all in-links are the same. Imagine two websites link to yours. The one that's a popular resource related to your field with excellent reputation and rankings will have a greater impact on your own reputation than the other, which is a personal blog with no readers.

So you can already see that getting in-links from reputable sources is not an easy task. Hence reputation is hard to fake. It's not based on what keywords you optimise your website for, or what your HTML code looks like. It's not something you have direct control over.

You can proactively ask other website owners for links to yours. They may or may not accept. Or they will ask that you link back in return – in which case the link they gave you is of diminished value, because it was obviously a trade.

Remember – Google indexes billions of pages by scanning each web page and detecting links on the page to determine where to go and index next. Hence Google knows how each and every website is interconnected. It has powerful algorithms to determine patterns and allocate reputation.

Only when you have great content or offer something of real value will your website draw plenty of attention and get links coming in. This is why blogging is a great tool.

Your page-rank is also affected when people talk about you and link to your website from social circles such as Facebook and Google+. In this case, it's not other websites, but people talking about you. This is also a good indicator of reputation. Being involved and active in social media websites is a powerful method to boost your page rank – and ultimately your website rankings in search engines.

Videos are excellent for building page rank because they're easy to consume and visitors generally enjoy videos. Creating regular videos is a good way to help your website's rank improve. Having a YouTube channel for your practice and uploading videos regularly is a good way for your website to start ranking higher. . You can read about YouTube strategies in the "Getting social" chapter.

Websites where people can leave reviews about your business are also very important. Encourage reviews to be left on your Google+ Local page. Make sure you respond positively to all reviews, including any negative ones. This is covered in the next chapter.

SEO dangers

You must take care not to abuse SEO. In the past, many opportunist business owners resorted to unethical SEO practices (known as black-hat SEO) to force improvement their rankings, trying to trick Google – instead of offering what human visitors will value.

Such activity results in bad experiences for Google's users. Imagine you search for a massage therapist and you get listings for unrelated or maybe even undesired websites, just because they'd figured out what you would be searching for.

For this reason, Google frowns upon such practices and the consequence is that these websites will get black-listed or banned altogether from Google.

Here are some black-hat techniques to avoid:

- Using hidden text or links. These could be hidden using the same colour as the page background so as to appear invisible to the public, but remain visible to Google crawlers.

- Using techniques to artificially increase the number of in-links to a page by buying and selling links with the main aim of increasing rankings in results pages.

- Using link farms to create masses of site links. These often lead to links between unrelated and therefore irrelevant pages.

- Excessively cross-linking between websites to inflate the apparent popularity.

- Cloaking: delivering different pages contents to the Google crawler and human visitors.

- Doorway pages – pages optimised for a keyword but that automatically redirect the user to another website.

- "Mousetrapping" – disabling the "back" button on a web browser, presenting a stream of excessive pop-up ads, or even re-setting a browser homepage.

- Duplicate content. Identical or very similar pages that can be accessed from different URLs that haven't been prepared properly.

- Misuse or cyber-squatting of competitor domain names or name typos, for example: microsofr.com

- Spamming forums and blogs with bogus comments and links.

- Excessive outbound links to websites that use high-risk techniques or spam.

- Link hoarding: getting as many inbound-links while giving out few outbound-links.

Your web developer or SEO consultant will be able to guide you through this minefield.

Local SEO

For a private practice like yours, one of the best SEO strategies lies in the "local" nature of your business.

Imagine you're a podiatrist in Denver, Colorado, USA. Would it be worthwhile to target "podiatry" as a keyword?

For starters, when you search for "podiatry" in Google, there are 11 million results[13]. This gives you an indication of your search engine competition, where you want to get to page 1.

Secondly, let's assume that somehow you managed to get your website to rank #1 for this keyword. It would be possible if you dominated social media, provided exceptional content and resources and received more in-links than all the state and national associations put together (and Wikipedia)... But for sake of argument, let's pretend that you managed to get there.

Who would your visitors be? Would they be people from a 20km radius of your practice? With such a big reach via such a generic and difficult keyword, you would be attracting visitors from all around the world. It would also mean that your content is inherently suitable for these target users – otherwise you couldn't possibly rank as such.

As a result, I (from Melbourne, Australia) can find your website, but would never be a client – since there are more podiatrists in local proximity to me. I would hit the back button and try a more localised search, such as "podiatrists in Melbourne" (220 thousand results) or narrow it further to my town "podiatrists in Essendon" (16 thousand results).

Your SEO effort has just been wasted.

---

[13] This is the number of results I get, when conducting this search from Melbourne, Australia. Your results may be different, since Google considers your location when you search.

By the way, searching for "podiatrists in Denver, Colorado" returns 32 thousand results. This is a more manageable level of competition than the original 11 million!

> The SEO strategy for a private practice business like yours needs to be focussed primarily on location-based keywords.

What percentage of searches is local?

Marissa Mayer, one of the main people responsible for "Local" at Google (now working for Yahoo), claimed that 20% of the searches on Google made via desktop browsers are local. This number goes up to 40% when talking about mobile searches (data from 25 May 2011[14]).

More important than this is the conversion rate (people who purchase) after performing a local search is very high; 43% of the users that performed local search actually contacted and/or visited the business. And from the overall local searchers, 22% made a purchase (data from 21 April 2011[15]).

These numbers are higher nowadays (as you would expect), and they vary from country to country and for different search engines. But the trend is clear.

[14] http://blog.kelseygroup.com/index.php/2011/05/25/20-of-google-searches-are-local-40-on-mobile/
[15] http://searchengineland.com/att-43-percent-of-local-mobile-searchers-walk-through-the-door-74198

Not just search engines

Local search is also relevant for maps and directories. You may have noticed when using a smart phone's map app that certain businesses can be found simply by searching for them near you (e.g. a bank or a coffee shop). Getting your practice listed here is crucial for your business.

Getting help

Properly designed and developed websites go a long way towards good search engine listings. Coupled with good content, your website may not need additional SEO to get to the first page of search results for your keywords. Many websites built and maintained by PracticePulse achieve great rankings by themselves. All the technical requirements for good SEO are already in place via the PracticePulse platform. However, here are some cases where you may need SEO help:

- Your website (and/or domain name) is new and it hasn't yet gained traction in search engines.
- You have a high level of competition online (or offline).
- There aren't enough people searching for your business or services directly.
- You want to promote the sale of specific services or products.
- You've been blacklisted from search engines for some reason and you don't know why.
- You're starting to lose your ranking due to changes in how search engines work or what your competition is doing to get higher (pushing your rank down).

> SEO is generally something you should get professional help with. Not only is it complex at the best of times, it's possible to end up in a worse position than where you started.

As a result of a successful SEO campaign, you can expect an increase in visits to your website. It will also result in an increase on the average time spent on your website and average number of pages viewed – since the visitors coming to your website are better targeted / qualified.

When choosing an SEO professional, look for someone who's passionate. He/she needs to understand the latest changes in algorithms and offer excellent advice. A very valuable skill to have is the ability to connect the dots in the results of an SEO campaign; attributing the results to the right actions means that the campaign can be further tweaked in the right direction.

Remember that SEO results cannot be guaranteed. There are only varying levels of SEO success. If anybody (outside of Google) knew exactly how Google worked, the knowledge could be used to manipulate the system. Hence such information is fiercely guarded. SEO professionals are good at knowing what "Google prefers" and how to prepare for it. Different SEO professionals will achieve different levels of success for different campaigns.

Lastly, expect an SEO campaign to take several months. This time is required to analyse, implement, test, measure and tweak the campaign continuously – to see what's working and what's not. Once a change is made somewhere, your website needs to be re-indexed by Google and that doesn't happen immediately.

Email marketing

With the advent of social media and all the records it breaks when it comes to marketing prowess, you may think that email marketing is dead.

But you'd be wrong. Because of the social media noise, the inbox gets more attention. Email will live longer than you think: it remains among the strongest online activity around the globe, with users expected to reach 3.8 billion by 2014 (up from 2.9 billion in 2010). Email is the preferred method of commercial communication by 74% of all online adults.

Email is a great lead generation and nurturing tool. People forward emails to others; it's the original medium for things to go "viral". People share great offers and interesting information. You can include excellent call-to-action in your email.

Even though 25% of recipients complain they dislike marketing clutter in their inbox, 40% claim to enjoy getting lots of marketing emails from favourite brands each week[16]. 20% spend an hour or more per week opening and browsing marketing emails.

However, most people simply don't know how to do it right. One-shot advertising or messaging is ineffective for you and frustrating for the recipient. You may think that your emails are "special" and worthy of attention, but it's just junk mail – unless you have their permission.

---

[16] http://www.bluekangaroo.com/media/ChoozOn-Blue_Kangaroo_Survey_on_Marketing_Emails_August_2012.pdf

Your intent with email marketing should be to build a long-term relationship so that you can have an active role in your readers' lives and wellbeing. With such intent, your emails are more likely to be opened and read.

> Studies indicate that up to 7 exposures are required before someone responds to your marketing email.

Besides lead generation and nurturing, email marketing is also excellent for keeping in touch with existing clients. Any businessperson or marketer can tell you that it's much easier to sell to someone who has purchased from you before than sell to someone new.

Very few private practice owners are using regular emails to keep in touch with their clients and prospects – mostly because it falls in the "too hard" category like everything else.

Why? Because most practice owners don't have a cheap, consistent and reliable system in place to stay in touch with existing and prospective clients.

> As your email list grows, so will your practice volume and income. Read that a few times and let this statement really sink in.

What you need

Firstly, you need to obey the rules. There are legal obligations around sending unsolicited emails. There are also a bunch of common sense rules around email etiquette. Not playing nicely can make you and your practice look bad and get you in hot water.

The next thing you need is an email list; i.e. a list of email addresses that you will send to and some software for sending mass emails. Preferably, one that is based in the cloud – not Outlook installed on your computer (see the resources section at the end of the book).

You will need great content and offers to send out. These will need to be written carefully, following best practices to ensure that they're opened and read, rather than getting deleted or caught up in spam filters.

Lastly, you will need a platform that can manage your email list and send them emails at one go. Check out the resources section of this book for ideas. If you have a PracticePulse website, these features are already built in.

> There's a good chance you're already collecting email addresses from your clients or prospects. There's also good chance that you're not doing it regularly or you aren't doing anything with your list (yet).

Your email list

Your email list can have many names:

- Newsletter subscribers / sign-ups
- Website members
- Email database
- Email recipients

- Marketing list

Essentially, it's a list with names and email addresses of people who want to receive communication from you. This is different from your fans or followers in social media, or visitors to your website.

Even a list as small as 100 focussed recipients can produce a solid profit stream for your business while creating genuine relationships with your community – if you're focussed and send them communication they'll value.

How do you get a list of email addresses that you can send your news and offers? The answer is: "build it". Creating remarkable content (web pages, blog posts, eBooks, newsletters etc.) is your first step in building your email list. Then you can proactively get permission and add recipients to your list by means of an incentive (or call-to-action).

Do you have permission?

Remember, the key is that the recipients in your email list must have given you permission to send them emails. This is called "opting in". When someone opts in, they're clear on what types of emails you will send them and they're happy to receive them. This is why email marketing is sometimes known as "permission marketing". It's one of the best forms of inbound marketing you can do.

> "The first rule of permission marketing is that it's based on selfishness: Consumers will grant a company permission to communicate only if they know what's in it for them."
> ~ Seth Godin

Do you have an incentive?

Your email list can include past and existing clients as well as leads and prospects. Getting email addresses is generally a simple matter of asking for them. In any case, you need to offer an incentive to someone if you want their permission to get your emails into their inbox.

Your incentive needs to be:

1. Something you can provide easily via this medium.
2. Something they'll value, want and look forward to.

Here are some examples of what you can offer as an incentive for people to give you their email address:

- Member-only content
- Practical information
- Free courses (e.g. webinar, video etc.)
- Special offers or discounts
- EBooks covering a specific topic of interest
- How-to videos
- Downloadable articles, whitepapers, reference sheets
- Interviews
- Regular contests, puzzles or games

It's critical to have a clear purpose when asking for an email address. Simply saying, "Enter your email address here for updates" won't get anyone excited. Your incentive should give visitors a reason to look forward to your emails. Take a moment to think about what you can offer.

Collecting email addresses

Now that you have your incentive in place, you now need a means of capturing name and email addresses of visitors who are interested. Best way to do this is with a "lead capture form". This is a short form on your website that enables visitors to submit their details into your database. Your website should be configured to handle this information and store it.

Besides using a lead capture form, you can also manually collect email addresses via your new client form. You may refer to it as a "patient intake form" in your practice, where you gather information about each new client that comes in for treatment. Make sure you have a field for email address, right after name and contact details. Include your incentive here (as before); don't be shy – ask to add them to your email list.

You can also invite subscribers through your social networks. Pretty much anywhere you get visitors, you can ask for email addresses. Again, ensure your incentive is clear.

Email marketing lists degrade by about 25% each year, due to readers losing interest, moving away or getting new email addresses. Growing your email marketing list should be a priority in your practice.

Barriers to collecting email addresses

People don't generally like to give out their email addresses, fearing an onslaught of spam. So be upfront; clarify what your emails will contain, how frequently they will be sent and of course what's in it for the recipient (your incentive). Tell them that you will not share their email address with anyone else, you won't be spamming them with irrelevant stuff and they can unsubscribe at any time; let them know that they're in control.

Another key barrier is complex online forms – some websites ask a willing user to jump through hoops to supply his or her email address. Make the process easy, with as few clicks as possible.

Double opt-in vs. single opt-in

Having a subscriber sign up form to collect emails on your website is great – however, pretty much anyone can put in any information that they want. If bogus email addresses or someone else's email address were supplied, your email list would start to fill with useless information. In a worst-case scenario, you could be sending spam to unsuspecting recipients because their email address was supplied without their consent.

To prevent this, the concept of "double opt-in" is used. Once your website captures an email address, it would send a "verification" email to the address just supplied. This email would contain a special link and message stating "please click on this link to verify that you want to sign up". After this, if the user does click on this link, you have not only successfully verified that the email address is real but the subscriber really wants to receive emails from you in the future and is more likely to engage with you.

The opt-in step may mean fewer signs-ups, but your list will be much cleaner and your chance of getting into spam trouble will be eliminated.

What to send

OK, now that you've started building your subscriber base, what emails do you send to them? What do you say? Well, whatever it is, it must be relevant to your subscribers' interests. What are your audience's pain points? How can you best deliver the solutions they need? If you don't know what this is, make sure to find out.

ENewsletters

A regular newsletter ("regular" being the key word here) should aim to educate the reader with relevant information. Such clinical content with topics related to your main services and offerings helps the reader in their day-to-day lives and makes your newsletter valuable.

Effective newsletters get personal – include an introduction and updates. Follow with authority-building content that shows your expertise and success as a private practice owner. You also want to include connection content (such as new staff, new services and social events) that helps the reader identify and connect with you, and get to know you better.

Newsletters are great for building your brand and associating a positive sentiment. You can leverage your blog posts by including summaries in your newsletter and driving traffic to your blog. You should try to raise interest at every opportunity and link back to your website as appropriate to increase visitors.

Whatever works for you, make sure that you do it regularly. Readers will expect a format that they're used to. The clinical (or professional) content you include should be of excellent quality. Aim to leave your readers thinking "I can't believe this is free information".

Email blasts

Besides newsletters, you can also send offers and promotions (as long as these are acceptable in your profession) as an email blast. To avoid email overload, you can include these within your newsletters; however, most offers will need special attention and are better off being sent as a solo message. Sometimes newsletters dilute your call-to-action because of their content value, and you'd be better off sending a mail-out with only your offer. Here are examples of what you can send:

- Promotions
- Event reminders
- Relevant seasonal or topical offers
- Gift certificates or coupons.

The rule of thumb for your email communication is to include one pitch (promotional message) for every 3 educational / informational messages / newsletters.

Getting personal

Remember that you have a special relationship with your clients, being a health and wellness provider. Accountants and lawyers couldn't hope to have relationships with their clients like you can. You can afford to (and should) get personal and informal in your email and newsletter communications. Don't be boring and monotonous. Talk as if you're talking to a friend.

You can start your newsletters with a welcome message for your new clients. You can use first names if you like, without violating privacy laws. This shows that you care about your new patients and creates authority that your practice is growing and is the correct place to be going.

You can introduce a new (or existing) employee to help clients and prospects get to know them. This can also be quite fun while building stronger relationships with your staff.

Where appropriate, you can showcase a client (or patient) of the month. This can be used to publicly highlight achievements or inspirational stories and praise the outcomes. You can also include testimonials too. Testimonials are very powerful tools and should be included in your newsletters. Of course, you should first check with your governing bodies that this is OK.

Besides showcasing clients or patients, you can showcase other professionals, especially if you get (or want to get) many referrals from them. Check with them first, and get them involved in your write up to make sure that what you say about them suits them too.

Include photos in your newsletters. These can be of you and your staff, events, clients or of anything that is relevant. Photos are great for breaking up chunks of text and also adding a personal touch. You can even consider including a regular headshot of yourself (especially if you work solo).

If you're asked the same questions over and over, include them in your newsletter. You can of course add them to your website also. Besides FAQ, you can also encourage readers to ask questions related to their conditions and provide answers in your newsletters. Readers will look forward to reading your answers to their questions in each newsletter.

Encourage communication; ask their opinions about a topic or hold a contest and give something away. Remember to thank readers for taking the time to get involved.

Add local news into your newsletter. You're a part of the community and what happens in your community affects everyone in it. Write about your involvement in and contributions to your community.

Feel free to include your personal views, ideas and wins. Having a regular clinical column in your newsletter is great, but make an effort to personalise every communication and build relationships. It's not always about what you do and offer. It's also about you. It may seem unnecessary, but your clients and prospects will appreciate it. Have fun with it – it doesn't have to be a chore for you or a bore for your readers. Just don't ramble – stay on topic.

> With relationship comes retention.

Planning ahead

When sending newsletters, rhythm and regularity is key. You may find that once a month is all you have time for, but ideally it should be more regular. Don't forget to set the correct expectations with your readers. Telling them that you will send "monthly newsletters" and then bombarding them every 2 days with offers is a good way to lose subscribers.

Check before you send

The last thing you want is to find out that the call-to-action link in your latest newsletter is broken or took the reader to the wrong page on your website.

Silly mistakes happen all the time. We're only human. It's a good idea to not only run a spell and grammar check, but also get a colleague to read over your email and check links before sending it out to your precious subscribers. Your marketing email software will have a feature to "send a test email" before committing the broadcast. Send yourself a test email and check it thoroughly from your inbox.

Also check that what you're sending is valuable to the readers. If not, change it.

Have a "no spam" policy

Spam is simply unsolicited, irrelevant or inappropriate messages sent on the Internet to a large number of recipients. It's generally associated with scammers and shoddy marketers. Best policy: don't send unsolicited email – period.

> Never send spam. It's bad for business.

Composing your marketing emails

A well-written plain text email can perform just as well, if not better, than a highly designed email with tons of graphics and colours. It's been proven over and over again that without great content, subscribers will stop opening and start deleting your emails. Then they'll unsubscribe.

Writing great marketing email copy takes courage and practice. Most of us are not used to writing like this, and we need to get comfortable with marketing copy. By the way, "copy" simply refers to the text you write.

The email subject line

The subject of your email is very important – it's the first thing your readers see in their inbox. It's your first and most crucial opportunity to grab attention and have your email opened. Take the time to craft your subject line carefully.

The subject line must be clear and catchy. Including action words helps. For example:

- "Stretch to improve your fitness"
- "Make time for health"
- "Ready for the ski season?"
- "Discover the real truth about…"

Raising curiosity also works well, such as:

- "The most surprising remedy to lethargy…"
- "A major breakthrough in…"
- "In the next 8 weeks, you could be…"
- "How many times have you said to yourself…?"

Your subject lines must relate to your email copy. It's no good getting the reader interested enough to open your email if its content doesn't fulfil on its promise.

To make it more challenging, the subject must be short. You can only see so many characters of the subject line before it is cut off with a "..." in your inbox.

The email contents

Now that you got your email opened, you want to get user engaged enough to click your links. We've already established that relevancy of your content is important. We've also established that you need to have a mix of educational, personal and sales content in your eNewsletter. Your promotional email blast will have a different focus.

Your opening greeting should use the recipient's name, like "Hi, Dennis". Just like your subject line is important, the first few lines of your email copy should also be considered carefully. You need to demonstrate relevance to the subject line and to your reader.

Keep your emails concise and compelling. Reduce ~~unnecessary~~ words. Use language that a 5th grade student can understand and address your readers' needs. Use headings and bullet points to break up your copy and draw attention.

After demonstrating value, focus on a single CTA (call-to-action) per email, such as "Click here to make an appointment today". Use actionable language in your CTA. Try to keep your main message or CTA near the top, so it can be seen without scrolling down. Don't confuse the reader with multiple CTAs, such as asking reader to call you, fill out surveys and tell their friends about your new treatment rooms.

If you're including an offer, make it worthwhile. Encourage readers to share your offer with their friends to spark a viral effect. Having a lame offer will make you look bad.

Images that you use should be resized to the correct height and width before you upload and insert them into your email body. Uploading a high resolution image which you scale down within the email body still results in a large download. Considering that many readers will be on mobile devices, you want fast downloads. Keep image file sizes low.

Email design

Remember, content is more important than design. Plain text emails sometimes work better than emails with great design. Sometimes great design takes attention away from what you're trying to present. Hence you should opt for simplistic designs that can be read easily. Most of the time, a template design is perfect for your needs.

Consistency of your email design is of significant importance – recipients will recognise your emails when they arrive. You should have a banner across the top, with your colours and logo.

Call-to-action buttons or links should be easily identifiable and clear as to their intent and purpose.

Other must-haves in your email design are:

- Contact details (telephone and address) displayed at the top. Reader should be able to see it without scrolling down the email.

- Unsubscribe link at the bottom (or a link to help readers manage their subscription).
- Links to send (forward) the email or newsletter to a friend.
- Links to your appointment request forms

To comply with spam laws, you should also note the following.

- Don't send false/misleading information.
- Don't use deceptive subject lines
- Clearly identify adverts

Keeping your list clean

Where do your emails go?

Expect to lose about 25% of your email marketing database every year. Your recipients' email addresses change as they change jobs, they unsubscribe (opt-out) from your email communication or mark your emails as spam once, thereby teaching their email program to ignore your emails thereafter.

As a result, your emails could be bouncing back or flagged as spam without ever reaching your intended audience.

In an attempt to cut down junk email floating around in cyberspace, email servers are often programmed to detect "repeat offences" and then "blacklist" them. This means that there is a possibility that even your good emails bound for people who are waiting for them could get blocked after a while.

So it's a great idea to keep your email marketing database clean from any invalid or undeliverable email addresses and stop sending to anyone who has reported your emails as spam. This is something that good mass email sending software can do for you.

Opt-outs are fine

You've already made sure that you're only collecting email addresses for people that want to hear from you in the first place. Besides this, simply make sure that anyone who wants to unsubscribe or opt-out can do so easily. This helps you to keep your list clean – there's no business sense in sending someone emails if they no longer want to hear from you, whatever their reason.

Staying out of the spam folder

In an effort to weed out spam from your inbox, most email software use techniques to detect emails that look like spam. The detection filters are getting better all the time, but every now and again some spam can creep through.

Unfortunately, inverse to this, sometimes good emails get caught up in spam filters because they "look" like spam. According to different sources, up to 20% of legitimate emails end up in spam folders. Here are some tips to avoid this issue:

- Only use permission-based opt-in email addresses and send anticipated, relevant messages.
- Don't use ALL CAPS in your email or the subject line.
- Don't use spam trigger words like "free", "work from home", "you have won", "buy direct", "affordable", "money back" etc. You get the idea.
- Avoid excessive use of exclamation marks!!!
- Spell check your email before sending.
- Don't send emails to undeliverable addresses (covered earlier).
- Ask your readers to add your email address to the "safe sender list" to avoid getting caught in spam filters in the future.
- Include a clear unsubscribe link.
- Ensure that everyone who wants to unsubscribe is assisted with this request.

There are also a bunch of technical precautions you can take, but your web developer will need to worry about those.

Micro-targeted communication

There's plenty of opportunity for one-on-one relationships that you should build using email. For example, you probably have the birth dates of all your clients; why not enter these into a calendar (Google calendar is excellent) and send them an email or call them up on their birthday? This is so easy to do and does wonders for building personal relationships with people.

You can send your clients gift certificates and "thank you" emails. Thank you emails are twice as engaging as general marketing emails; you can thank a client for trusting you with their needs or sending you referrals. You can email clients when they haven't shown up in a while. Show that you care.

This is just old school marketing. You can use your software and tools to perform these regularly and easily.

Your VIP referrers

You may have a small group of targeted referrers, such as insurance companies, physicians and other professionals. You should aim to communicate more personally with these people, rather than simply sending them a regular newsletter. Your newsletter, blog and website can establish your authority and credibility, but regular personal contact with them is required to keep them referring you clients.

To make things more interesting, you can create a personalised webpage on your site with your crafted message, with a unique, personal URL. Personalised URLs are covered later in this book.

Mobile marketing

Mobile marketing refers to application of mobile technology for location and time based promotions. Mobile usage is at an all-time high and continues to grow. With access to smart devices that can connect to the Internet, increase social reach and provide on-demand research on any topic, the mobile user is a different breed of consumer.

Here are a few key statistics, from various sources:

- Mobile internet usage is projected to overtake desktop internet usage by 2014, with 7 billion mobile devices connected to the Internet.

- There will be almost 800 million mobile-only Internet users by 2015.

- There are 5 times as many mobile phones as PCs in the world. Globally, there are 4 births and 39 mobile phones sold per second.

- 91% of adults have their phone within arm's reach 24/7. 83% of text messages are read within 3 minutes of being delivered. 98% are opened.

- 81% of smartphone users have done product research via a smartphone. 79% of smartphone consumers use their phone to help with shopping.

- 95% of smartphone users have looked for local business information. 90% of shoppers use their smartphone to check for contact, location and business hours information.

- 2 in 3 buyers would rather use their mobile device to seek product information, than to ask a store employee.

- 9 out of 10 mobile searches lead to an action, and over half purchase. 88% lead to action within a day (immediate needs).

These stats will surely be obsolete soon, since this is a rapidly changing landscape. But you can see the importance of being ready for mobile for your practice. Mobile users are on a steep rise and they have a higher propensity for action than desktop Internet users.

The "mobile user"

People don't just "surf" on mobile devices. Surfing is easier on larger screens; if a user is checking something out on a small screen with slower Internet speeds, it's generally because he/she is ready to take some action and their mobile device is convenient.

Shopping inspiration can come any time. Recent market research shows that people like the idea of shopping with their mobile devices, and almost two-thirds of device owners actually expect to be shopping via their mobile device over the coming years[17]. Waiting until they get to a computer is not necessary.

Smartphones are more trusted than store assistants when it comes to asking questions about a particular product. It also follows that these people who use their smartphones to do product research are likely to spend 25% more in-store than someone who doesn't research.

Much of this research is based around product details, reviews, price comparisons, promotional offers, finding location or store directions and hours.

Does this mean that there's a million people out there waiting by their mobile devices to break down your practice doors? Perhaps not yet. However, you can see the trends and the importance of being prepared in your business. Your mobile-friendly website will be as important as your traditional website, if not more so.

---

[17] Latitude, "Next-Gen Retail: Mobile and Beyond"

And in the meantime, making a mobile website is still an excellent way to grow your business from a lead-generation, branding, and marketing-outreach perspective...

Your mobile-optimised website

In case you were under the impression that all this was somehow optional, here's another interesting statistic: 6 out of 10 people believe that having a mobile presence is key to their positive perception of a brand; they not only want you to make your website mobile, they demand it.

- 67% of users are more likely to purchase a product or service from a mobile-friendly site.
- 74% of users say they're also more likely to return to a site in the future if it's mobile-friendly.
- 52% of users said a bad mobile experience made them less likely to engage with a company.
- 61% of users want to be able to click-to-call a business from their website while on their mobile device; 54% are looking to send an email.

There are some special considerations when preparing a mobile optimised website for your practice. You need to remember that mobile users have different needs than the usual desktop users.

Mobile users typically want quick reference information, rather than detailed research into specific topics. The latter is more convenient to do while at a desktop computer. If you have a ton of content on your website, your mobile-optimised website may need to have only a subset of these, while keeping focus on things like your location and contact details, business hours and appointment forms.

For this reason, it makes sense to have two versions of your website – one for general Internet users and a mobile-optimised version for mobile users. However, note that this doesn't mean that you need to maintain two different websites. Speak with your web developer about how you can serve a different version of a website for different users (i.e. mobile), while only maintaining the one website.

> Because of their distinct focus and smaller display screens, there are special design considerations for mobile-optimised websites.

On any website, the visitor should always be able to answer the questions "where am I?" and "what can I do here?" While on a mobile device, these questions are even more emphasised. The design of a mobile-optimised website needs to be very simple. You should still allow for your branding (logo and colours), but besides that, think "vanilla". Web pages with heavy images and design elements simply get in the way.

Stick to essential content and functionality. Mobile users are generally multitasking (shopping, watching TV, walking) while they are on your website. Let them get to the things they need fast. As mentioned, consider providing a smaller selection in your menus and options. Avoid using horizontal menus; they may not fit across the screen. Use large buttons and clear links so they can be "tapped" easily with a finger.

Ensure that your mobile phone links through to the phone application, so the visitor can place a phone call straight from your website.

> Discuss with your web developer what needs to be done to mobile-optimise your website.

One point, while we're on the topic: there are free and paid online services that "translate" or "convert" your existing website for mobile presentation. Most of these do a bad job and you should avoid them. If you have a WordPress website, there are design themes you can use for your website that are mobile optimised at the same time (known as responsive design) – these are a good option. Your web developer can also ensure that your website is optimised for mobile.

Besides your mobile-optimised practice website, mobile marketing will also touch on social media and PPC advertising. These are covered separately in other parts of this book.

What about SMS?

SMS (texting) is by no means new technology and it's had its wild ride. Remembering that 9 out of 10 adults have their phone within arm's reach at all times and 8 out of 10 text messages are read within 3 minutes of delivery, it remains a great medium of communication.

Big companies with recognised brands (e.g. Coca Cola, Nike) can still get excellent responses and ROI from targeted SMS campaigns such as national competitions. SMS is rarely successful for the average small business as a means of generating leads. Users don't want to receive ongoing marketing SMS messages.

There are definite opportunities and advantages with SMS – it's a very personal medium that users clearly find extremely important.

Hence use of SMS for your practice marketing needs to be done right. Interrupting users with irrelevant messages isn't a good idea.

In your practice, use SMS for doing more with existing clients, instead of getting new leads.

The best application of SMS in your practice that's completely acceptable (or even appreciated) is for appointment reminders. Granted, this isn't marketing, but it's good use of technology to reduce no-shows and help your clients meet their needs. Sending an SMS in this case is often better than calling them up.

You can also use SMS to follow up after treatment, with a simple message such as "How do you feel today after your treatment?"

With appointment reminders and follow-up messages, make sure that you check for any reply messages.

In specific circumstances, sending an SMS with time-sensitive ultra-special offer with exceptional value to a targeted group can work well. However, each business is different – you should experiment and start small, gauging response every step of the way. You'll soon get a feel for which clients this works and who to leave alone.

Collecting mobile numbers

Before you can send SMS, you need to have your clients' mobile (cell) number. You can simply collect this on your new client or patient intake form.

How to do it

Sending SMS from your mobile phone is straightforward enough. However, if you'll be sending messages regularly, you'll need an easier method.

If you use client/patient management software in your practice, it may already have feature to send SMS via your computer. This way you can save and reuse popular messages and access your recipients' numbers easily.

Alternatively, there are many online SMS sending services available which you can subscribe to. These are generally subscription or credit based. Check out the resources section of this book.

Just note that when some online systems send SMS messages the recipient can't see the sender's number (because it wasn't actually sent from a phone). As a result, they can't reply. Make sure that the system you pick allows you to nominate an existing mobile number, so even when you send SMS online, you can collect replies on a phone.

Location-Based Marketing

Location-based marketing is marketing to people based specifically on their location. Your smartphone has a GPS device built in which can connect you to where you are. So this can be leveraged to help you find a product or service nearby when you need it.

This is of obvious interest to you, yes? It's a good way to get people through your practice doors as a local business.

Suffice to say that for now, ensure that the Google+ Local Page and Facebook Page for your practice have been set up and properly populated with accurate information about your practice location and contact details.

These are specifically covered in the "Getting social" chapter.

QR codes

QR stands for "quick response". It's a form of printed code (like the barcode on the back of this book) that has some information embedded in it which can be decoded and actioned by a smartphone. An example of a QR code is shown on the right.

When scanned using the camera on a smartphone, the information encoded in a QR code can do things like:

- Display a URL
- Show your location in Google Maps
- Save your personal or practice contact details into the phone's directory (having a QR code with your practice contact details on your website's contact us page or business card is a good idea)
- Initiate an SMS or email message to be sent by the user
- Initiate a telephone call to a number you specify
- Create a calendar event

All this, simply by pointing your smartphone camera to a code made up of little black blocks.

Most smartphones can't scan QR codes by default – a QR code scanner app (freely available) needs to be installed. I like to use "Scanlife" to read QR codes. Search for it in your app store. There are loads of others you can find simply by searching for "QR code scanner".

One disadvantage of using QR codes is that they are still somewhat a mystery for most of the public. Though they've likely noticed them around, most people don't know what they are, let alone how to install an app and scan the code.

But this too is changing; it's worth considering or experimenting with QR codes because they are so easy to produce and distribute. It can be great resource to grow your Facebook fan base, grow your subscriber list or promote special offers.

The advantage is that you can convey a lot of information with a single scan, saving many keystrokes on a handheld device. It bridges the physical and digital worlds. It's convenient for the user and arouses curiosity.

How to create QR codes

There are many free online resources for creating QR codes. You simply need to choose what you want the QR code to do (e.g. open a web page or save your contact details to the user's phone) and then supply the information to encode. You can then grab the produced image (QR code) and print it wherever you want. Take a look at the resources section of this book to find online QR code creation services.

Using QR codes for marketing

One consideration is size and reliability. If you expect people to scan your code from afar, then it must be printed large enough that it can be recognised by the scanner app on a smartphone. If it's too small or not printed clearly, then scanners may not pick up the encoded message.

Once you have your QR code, always test it to make sure that it works before you publish it. Also remember that since QR codes are optimised for mobile devices, ensure that your website is mobile-friendly.

Mobile apps

Apps are the small software that you download and run from your smartphone. There is a lot of clutter in the mobile app stores – whether in Apple's App Store, or any one of the other online app market places. Stats also say that 1 in 4 apps are never used again, once downloaded.

Even though it's getting cheaper to have apps built these days, the average private practice has no such needs. You may have quiet spots in your appointment book and you think push notifications and proactive geo-targeted messages can reach nearby people quickly and offer them a timely discount. But, you can easily leverage social media, email marketing and SMS for a more cost effective solution.

Unless you have a strong case for getting an app (and you have discussed this with a consultant), save your money and time.

Pay-Per-Click: Paid advertising

We've already covered the importance of ranking well in search engines for the search terms that you want to be found for. We've also established that good content and SEO is an important long term strategy for getting good "organic" or "natural" ranking for your website.

However, you may want to consider alternate methods of getting qualified visitors to your website. Paid listing (also known as paid placements, pay-per-click or PPC) could be a good solution when:

1. Your website (and/or domain name) is relatively new and it hasn't yet gained enough traction.
2. You have too much competition and are finding it hard to rank well against them.
3. You want to target precisely the kind of visitors you want.
4. You need quick and effortless traffic to your website.

You've seen paid listings before – they appear along the very top or right hand side of Google search results. They also appear in the sidebar of Facebook. Someone has paid money to place those adverts in there, to be displayed when specific search terms are entered by the user. When you click on one of those links, you're taken to the page nominated by the advertiser.

Advantages of PPC

Better conversion rate: Visitors to your website arriving via a PPC link are more likely to convert into a client of your practice.

Website content, authority and structure aren't as important: While SEO attempts to earn traffic by virtue of content and authority, PPC simply buys traffic.

Easier: PPC is easier to set up and get results from in the short-term. But it's just as easy for your competitors, therefore eliminating the competitive advantage.

Disadvantages of PPC

PPC is advertising: 70-80% of people are more likely to click on natural listings rather than paid listings. Savvy users are staying away from adverts, since many of these links result in landing on some sales page with a form on it.

It's easy to be hooked on PPC: Like a drug of dependence, it's easy to be hooked on PPC for its short-term results. Although it takes longer, SEO offers lasting results.

PPC can cost more in the long run: Once an SEO campaign picks up pace, its return on investment increases over time. PPC remains a constant expense, as long as your competitors don't drive your costs up by bidding more than you for the same visitors.

Long-term performance: Paid

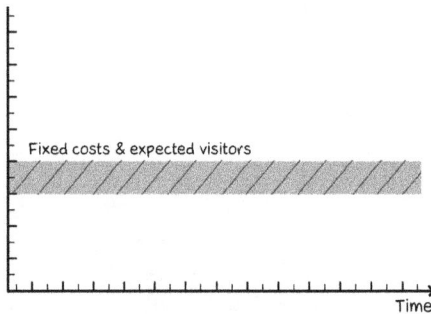

Fixed costs & expected visitors

Time

Long-term performance: Organic

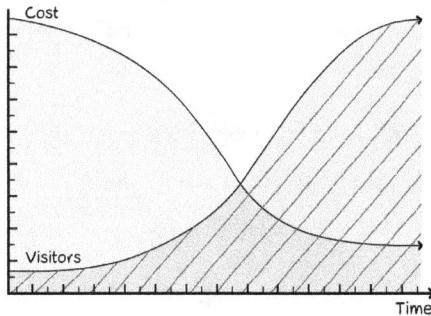

Cost

Visitors

Time

For example, assume you are paying $4 per click to bring a visitor to your website. If 1 visitor in 50 makes an appointment and comes in for treatment, then it has cost you $200 to get each client. Clearly, paid advertising could add up quickly, so it's not a viable long-term strategy.

A common misconception is that spending more on PPC will lead to higher organic rankings for your website. This has never been verified.

Another misconception is that PPC delivers positive results more quickly than SEO. While it's true that PPC does deliver quick results, whether these are positive or not is irrelevant; it's easy to spend lots of money on PPC and not get a single new client. There's still a lot of work to be done to achieve positive results.

How PPC works

There are several places you can pay to advertise your practice website. Most notable are:

1. Google AdWords
2. Facebook advertising

The basic premise is that you typically create your advertisements and "bid" for your placements. If you're happy to pay a higher premium for your placements, your adverts get shown more prominently and more often.

Your adverts would then get displayed to relevant users and you only pay the agreed amount if and when someone clicks on your advert. After clicking your advert, the user would be taken to your nominated webpage (where you intend on "converting" the visit into a client).

Variable pricing

You might be lured by the benefit that you only pay for your adverts if someone actually clicks on your advert in the first place – not by impressions (how many times it was displayed). However, note that all advertisements are typically auctioned. If you agree to pay more "per click", your advertisement would display higher than someone who targeted the same users but bid less than you.

There are several other factors that affect how much you would pay per click. If you paid a premium to list your advertisement at the top spot and no one has clicked on it after (say) 1000 impressions, then it could be deemed a "bad offer". Or if people click on your adverts, visit your website and return back to search results later, then it could be deemed that your website wasn't quite up to scratch and it didn't fulfil the user's need. In cases like these, you can find yourself actually paying a lot more to keep that top advertisement spot than someone else – i.e. another advertiser could in fact end up paying much less than you to be placed at the top, simply because they have a better offer or a better website.

This kind of mechanism helps reduce bad or forceful advertisers in an overall attempt to keep the user's experience pleasant. Hence simply paying for an advert isn't all there is to it – you still need to have a good strategy to make the most of your campaigns.

You also need to track your PPC budget and your return on PPC investment carefully. You could easily end up spending more than you make from your campaign.

Now that we've covered the basics, let's look at a few prominent PPC platforms. But before we do, please remember that PPC can be daunting when you first start: each platform does things a little differently, there are proprietary metrics to decipher and numerous segmenting and targeting options to understand. This is all before you even start bidding on anything. So take it nice and slow, start out with small campaigns first until you feel more confident.

Google AdWords

In Google's search results page, paid listings appear across the top and the right hand side of the page. They are identifiable with a pale yellow background.

Google's advertisement system is called AdWords.

AdWords is a very deep topic – entire books have been written about it. I'm only going to give you a basic overview, so you can decide to pursue AdWords (or not).

With AdWords, you'll be able to reach your clients at the right time – when they're looking for your services. Since you get to specify the search terms you want your ads to display with, you have a pretty good idea of what the user is looking for. Example: if you want to get more people into your Pilates classes in Sydney, you could create an AdWords campaign for the search term "Pilates in Sydney" or "Pilates classes Sydney". Now when someone searches for these keywords, your adverts could display in the paid listings area.

Sometimes you may want to trial AdWords campaign for the keywords that are already performing well for you. Why? Because it means that your website link will be seen on the page more than once. Chances are, if you're already ranking well, your AdWords ad campaign for those keywords will probably cost you less than what someone else would need to pay.

When creating (or editing) your campaign, Google will let you know the position your adverts will appear for your bid amount, based on your keywords and how many other practice owners are also bidding for those keywords. If none of your competitors are interested in advertising for those keywords, your campaign could end up very cost effective.

Google will also give you an indication as to how many people (on average) search for your target keywords and the number of impressions you can expect per month. What it can't tell you is how many people will actually click on your advert. That depends on how well your advert is written. What it also can't tell you is how many of the people that click on your link and go to your website will actually become your clients; that depends on how well you can convert them to buyers at your website. This is where your offer, design, content etc. play their role.

Remember to track your AdWords expenditure and review it regularly. You may find that you get results just as good by being in the second position, rather than outbidding everyone for the top position. With trial and error, you can soon get a good feel for it.

Getting started

To get started with AdWords, you just need a Google account. If you don't already have a Google account, you can get one for free here: **accounts.google.com/signup**

After that, you can go to your AdWords management console here: **adwords.google.com**

These are always changing, so Google provides ample instructions to help you along. Here are the basic steps:

Firstly, you need an excellent keyword list. Think about the keywords your clients are most likely to use – what are their biggest pain points? What do THEY search for? Remember that they may not speak your language and use your terminology when they search. A lot of thought goes into this step, so be prepared for some work.

You should include geo-targeting in your AdWords campaigns since any prospect who will become a client will most likely be a local – not from around the world. AdWords provides good tools to help you generate and select good keywords. It will also give you an indication as to how much competition you can expect for a keyword and also how many people are searching for it each month.

You generally want to select keywords that more people are searching for, as long as it's relevant to your offer. However, go back a step and consider whether someone searching for a particular keyword is likely to become a client.

High competition means that many other advertisers could be targeting those keywords – and you may need to pay a higher fee to get listed among them.

Google gives you an estimate of how much you can expect to pay for your listings. Get your calculator out and work out how much you are willing to pay. You don't want to pay more for your adverts than what they might make you in the long run.

Tracking your ads

As I mentioned earlier, it's very important to track not only your AdWords expenditure, but also your actual conversions: how many clients did you get from your AdWords campaign and how much money did you make from it?

Your AdWords account provides ample data to track your campaigns. You can couple this with your website usage data to derive more relevant information.

A practical idea is to have a page on your website with a special offer – one that only visitors from your AdWords campaign will see, since only your advert will click through to that page. When someone claims this offer, you will know that it came from your AdWords campaign.

You can later use the other data such as how many people came to that page, how long they stayed, how many more times they visited your website etc. to fine-tune your website and AdWords campaigns further.

Google AdWords Express

AdWords Express has been around nearly two years. It helps you to promote your business on Google Search and Maps. When people search your area for the products or services you provide, an ad for your business will appear above or beside their search results. Your business will also be marked with a pin on Google Maps, helping it stand out to potential clients.

Compared to AdWords, AdWords Express is an advertising solution geared more for local businesses, like yours. It's a simpler advertising platform – both to set up and maintain. Taking 5-10 minutes to complete, you can be up and running without even needing to think about keywords or starting bid prices.

Benefits of AdWords Express advertisements:

- Create an online ad quickly and easily.
- Pay only when people click your ad.
- Attract more local clients to your website; Google will automatically target your ads for you based on your geographical location.
- Minimal ongoing management necessary.
- Reach clients on desktop computers and mobile devices.
- Review the effectiveness of your ads in your dashboard.
- No need for keyword research and analysis.

However, its simplicity means you can get lazy and not achieve results as well as you can with regular AdWords. To get started, go here: **adwords.google.com/express**

Facebook advertising

Facebook has been experimenting with different advertising options. It seems that a new way to advertise on Facebook is released every month. Here are a few options that are currently available:

1. Facebook ads
2. Promoted posts
3. Promoted events
4. Custom audiences

Facebook advertising options are still relatively cheap since people are still new to it. However, this will likely change pretty soon.

Another benefit of Facebook advertising options is that unlike Google, Facebook knows a lot more about its users; it knows your gender, age, hobbies, friends, occupation, interests, likes and dislikes. This gives the advertiser an incredible level of targeting, unlike anything possible before.

Getting started

For best results, some of Facebook's advertising and marketing options require that you have a Facebook page for your business and that your business details have been correctly filled in. Others simply require a payment, similar to AdWords.

In any case, you will need a Facebook account to get started. Note that a Facebook account and Facebook Page (also known as a business page or a fan page) are different things. You can read about these later in this book.

Visit **facebook.com/advertising** to start your advertising campaign you can look for the "create an ad" links throughout Facebook.

The process of creating an ad can be daunting at first, but Facebook offers clear explanations and prompts along the way. We won't go into all the specifics here, since they're always changing.

Tracking your ads

Facebook provides good data to help you track your campaigns' performance. However don't just look at the numbers blindly. Try to work out the bigger picture: of the visitors you received at your website from your ad, how many became clients? For the 200 new likes you received on your Facebook page, how many are active and genuinely interested in your services? Simply looking at click through rates won't give you a very good indication.

Just like Google AdWords, you can end up spending a lot of money with Facebook ads. Remember that your investment must give you a greater return; otherwise it's not working.

Social Media

Having started out as a personal communication medium, social media has developed into an important tool that businesses large or small can't ignore.

Jane thought Paul's profile pic was cute
but didn't realise her mistake till the first date.

An online social network is much like your real social networks. It's comprised of your friends and your family, work colleagues and acquaintances. Social networks help you to stay in touch with people and make new connections. With online social networks, rather than seeing people face to face, you use tools such as Facebook, Google+, Twitter and many others.

Online social networks are great because they help you to discover what your connections are up to and share information, photos, videos and thoughts easily. It's convenient, useful and fun. This is why the world has taken to it so much.

Social media is so powerful that many countries around the world ruled under some form of dictatorship have outlawed or censored major social networks.

Part of the marketing puzzle

It's important to note that your social media strategy and activities will form a part of the same marketing puzzle. We've noted that pretty much everything you do in online marketing is interconnected. You can get good results by focussing on individual techniques such as email list building or creating great content, but there is a synergy that occurs with a multi-pronged strategy. For example, developing a great profile and being active in social media can mean your website (which is typically disconnected from your social networks) can start ranking higher as if by magic. Having a great blog and content can drive your social media interaction forward, feeding back into your marketing.

Think of it like your own online ecosystem. But you need to do the right things to grow and keep it healthy. Ubiquity and consistency is key.

As you become an authority in your field, you'll start getting recognition and traction. Having more people arrive at your website (mother ship) will ultimately lead to more new and repeat clients through your practice doors. Not only that, you'll have better relationships overall.

If you only use social media for hard-selling, you'll never achieve engagement and ultimately no sales. A Commscore/Facebook survey reported that Starbucks' Facebook followers purchased 38% more in-store than non-followers. This shows the connection between engagement and offline purchasing habits.

Just like most other online marketing activities, social media takes persistence and patience – maybe even more so. It also helps if you have a knack for it; just like networking in real-life. But it's not hard when you simply stick to a strategy.

Again, you can see the importance of an online strategy and commitment. Scattergun approach or hope isn't a strategy.

> There are no one-shot activities in an online strategy.

The good news is that there are excellent tools, guidance and support readily available.

Importance of social proof

People are now using social networks to discuss everything from what someone's cat brought home, to the customer service they received at their local department store. Businesses have realised that this medium of free and public speech presents them with threats *and* opportunities. Consumer sentiments about a business can quickly turn into public discussions, whether they like it or not. In a very short time, this has become a very powerful medium for shaping the way businesses do business; and it's the trend of the future.

It's no longer sufficient for a business to claim something – there is always someone out there who can verify or negate claims publicly. There have been many instances where global corporations have been humiliated by individuals when a cover-up story or a mishandled client had "gone viral" via social networks.

What people say about you or your business is "social proof". This also has a way of leaking out of social networks and into Google searches.

> You are who Google says you are.

You, as a local private practice owner, need to recognise the power of social networks and ensure that you represent yourself well, as well as engage with discussions in this social medium.

Your clients are going to be talking about you – will you be there to hear it and respond? What will people find out about you, before even contacting you for an appointment?

Social networks clearly influence buying behaviour. Coupled with the convergence of social networks and mobile technology and fuelled with consumers' insatiable appetite for information and trust in their friends' recommendations, you need to make social media strategy a priority in your practice. Social media is like turbo-charged word-of-mouth.

It's a marathon, not a sprint

Entrepreneur and public speaker Gary Vaynerchuk puts it: "Look at your social media strategy as a long distance marathon, not a sprint."

Networking events are great for meeting people who also want to network. But your clients don't want to be "networked" to, like they don't want to be sold to.

Local businesses that are run by friendly, caring, community focussed owners get and keep more clients and build more long-term goodwill than those who target short-term gains. As a buyer, you're not excited about a business's bottom line – you get excited about the interactions you have.

All the social norms and expectations for connecting in real life apply to connecting online. Remember, you can always take the interaction offline to connect with more meaning after the initial introductions through social media.

Throw a party

Think of your social media strategy more like hosting an open door party. There will be people you know, their guests and even random people who show up out of curiosity.

As a host, you should aim to show everyone a good time and try to spend time with each guest. You should converse, introduce people and offer drinks and finger foods. You should engage the shy individuals and encourage them to join in.

Most of your guests (known as "followers" or "fans" in social media speak) will already know that you run a private health practice. They may ask you related questions. Excellent! Discuss their concerns and answer their questions as appropriate. You may need to tell them to come see you on Monday.

> Offer free advice, tips and ideas; you're the expert in the room.

In fact, social media is a great place to distribute your published content. The nature of the medium makes it easy for your followers to take something of use and pass it onto their own friends, thereby giving you greater reach than you imagined.

It's not so much about the numbers. It's about relationships. Would you rather have 2000 followers on your preferred social media channel where none of them were interested in you or what you do, OR have 250 who become good friends, clients and referrers?

Most businesses that fail in social media don't understand it or take it seriously enough to build relationships – they treat it like a one night stand trying to score on the first date. Don't be that person; it could do your business more damage than good.

Switching analogies, being good at social media is like being good at singing. Like those shows on TV, people enjoy listening to people who have a good voice, can hold a tune and have flair about them.

As a business owner in private practice, you can tout messages, offers or push online interactions with people every day, but will people listen to you? Will they even notice you? Just like in singing, when it comes to social media some people have natural talent, others need practice. So don't be disheartened.

Facebook

Facebook is one of the best tools available in your social media toolkit for promoting your practice. It offers excellent opportunities for business when used correctly. Here are some Facebook stats you may find interesting:

- More than 1 billion monthly active users, more than 750 million active daily users with more than 1 trillion page views per month.
- Average time spent on Facebook is 8.3 hours per user per month (about 15% of total time spent online).
- 45% of 65+ year-old Internet users are on Facebook.
- More than 1.1 trillion Facebook "likes" since launch of likes, growing at 4.5 billion per day.

- 17 billion location-tagged posts since introduction of location tagging.
- 5 billion items are shared per day.
- More than 50% of Facebook users actually purchase from brands or businesses they follow online.

You shouldn't be surprised if businesses across all sectors soon state Facebook as their number one social media tool. We've already covered Facebook advertising earlier in this book, now we will look at how you can raise your profile online using Facebook.

If you are somehow completely new, Facebook is a social network that connects people. Anyone 13 years and older can sign up for free. After filling out your profile information and supplying details such as places you lived, went to school and worked, it will start suggesting people you may know. After you have a few "friends" on Facebook, it will examine your interactions with these people and offer you more intelligent suggestions as to who else may be your friend. Privacy is important, so no one can be your Facebook friend until you accept the invitation (and vice versa).

During your time on Facebook, you will most commonly view your News Feed (also known as home page). When one of your friends posts something about where they are or what they're doing, it appears on your News Feed. You can quickly skim down your News Feed and view the different posts, news and photos that your friends have shared. You can leave comments for them (and their friends) to see and participate in a discussion. You can also click on the thumbs-up "like", to let your friend know that you found their post or comments interesting. It's easy to get overwhelmed if you have a lot of Facebook friends, so you can fine tune how much of what you want to see and from whom.

Anything you post or share ends up on your Timeline. Everyone with a Facebook account essentially maintains his or her own Timeline. Your Facebook News Feed is simply an aggregate of recent posts and shares from you and your friends' Timelines, sorted with the most recent (or most popular) posts at the top. You can view your own Timeline to see all your own posts in the one place. Similarly you can view a particular friend's Timeline, which is great for reminiscing or browsing for something they've shared in the past.

All of this activity (likes, comments and shares) by people is inherently viral, since friend can see them and propagate by liking, commenting and sharing a post further to their own circle of friends.

Besides your friends, you can also follow certain channels for news and information called "Pages", created by Facebook users. A Page can be about anything, from celebrities or brands to small business marketing and personal fitness inspiration. If you find a Page that appeals to you, you can click on the "like" button to become a fan of that Page and have its updates fed through to your Facebook homepage.

Facebook for business

Facebook has exploded in popularity because it helps people to connect and communicate, even if they aren't logging in regularly. Businesses, celebrities, governments, brands and hobbyists have all taken notice and jumped on the Facebook bandwagon to get intimate with their audiences who have shown interest in them.

Facebook allows several other unique ways for people to share what is going on in their lives. For example, one can "check in" when they visit a particular venue, event or business to let their friends know that they were there. New features of Facebook (currently being rolled out) allow you to conduct focussed searches such as "friends who visited a chiropractor in Sydney" or even "friends of my friends who visited a physiotherapist nearby". You can also look up businesses directly, such as "podiatrists nearby". Known as Graph Search, this is Facebook's foray into Google territory as a search engine that takes cues from social activity and interaction data. The potential for small businesses is exciting.

You can see that your business could benefit from being on Facebook. Most of your patients and prospects are already there. You simply need to create a Facebook page for your practice.

Your Facebook Page

Every person who wants to use Facebook needs a personal account. Facebook's policy does not allow one person to create multiple Facebook accounts. In the early days, people started setting up separate accounts to promote their businesses, using the same profile and tools available for personal accounts. Facebook noticed this demand and introduced Facebook Pages.

Facebook Pages are designed for businesses, brands and other types of organisations. They offer different tools and profile settings to facilitate specific needs.

Your Facebook Page is locally discoverable – it can be searched for and found based on your business name or services you offer.

It helps you connect with the public, clients and staff. It allows you to broadcast without being "in-your-face" – you can reach large groups of people frequently with messages tailored to their interests. It even helps you understand your clients by giving you insights into their behaviours.

Just like with your own personal Timeline, you can post messages, updates, photos, events and more to your Page's Timeline. Only people who have "liked" your Facebook page will see these posts in their News Feed. In a sense, these people have given you permission to advertise to them. Your Facebook Page enables your business to interact socially with clients and prospects.

Creating a Facebook Page

Once logged into your personal Facebook account, you can visit **facebook.com/pages/create** to get started. You'll be guided through the process; however, you should pay particular attention to the following:

- Business type and category. You'll need to select "Local business".
- Complete contact details.
- Your "About" information/description, with link to your website.
- Cover photo and profile image for your practice.

The process of creating a Facebook Page is constantly evolving, but the guidance provided by Facebook is also getting better.

With the basics out of the way, consider the following:

- Get a name for your Page (i.e. custom URL).
- Who will be your Page administrators?

- Will you allow public posting to your Page's Timeline?

Although your Facebook Page's "About" tab will contain your contact details, it's a good idea to craft your cover photo so that these details are embedded into the image. If your telephone number is visible right within the header image, people won't need to look for it.

Getting a name for your Facebook Page

When you create a Page, Facebook assigns an arbitrary URL for it, containing a series of numbers. Instead of using this, you should claim a username (such as facebook.com/yourpracticename) for your Page as soon as you can.

After creating your Facebook Page, you can claim your username by visiting **facebook.com/username**. Note that there are some guidelines and restrictions around changing this username afterwards. Your best bet is to use your practice name or some abbreviated variation of it, considering factors such as competitors who may want a similar name.

Managing your Facebook Page

You can nominate other Facebook users as admins for your Page. Depending on their access level, admins can perform a variety of tasks within your Facebook Page, such as content creators, moderators and overall managers.

Since each admin must be a Facebook user already, there should never be a case where multiple people use the same account to manage a Page.

Note that if one of your Page admins posts something that repeatedly violates Facebook's Community Standards, the entire Page may be suspended. So only add admins who you can trust to represent your practice.

Converting a personal account to a Facebook Page

You may have unwittingly created a personal Facebook account in the past for your practice. Now that you know about Facebook Pages, do you need to start from zero? No – thankfully Facebook offers a Facebook Profile to Business Page Migration tool to make this process easy. Simply do a Google search for something like "Converting a personal account to a Facebook Page".

Multiple locations

If your business operates out of multiple locations, you'll need separate Pages for them. When it comes to local businesses, each Page represents a single address/location – even if they're part of the same business.

This is important later, when you want to enable visitors to "check in" at your clinics and be found for searches related to your location.

Posting to your Facebook Page

Posting to your Page is almost the same as posting to your personal Timeline. You simply supply your content (text, website links, photos, video etc.) and click "post".

However, as discussed earlier, your Page is for your business and people who'll see your posts are those who opted in to follow your posts. They have a certain expectation with regards to what you share. So save those irrelevant cat photos and political discussions to your personal Timeline.

Facebook gives you the option to post either as the Page admin or as yourself. Typically, you'll be posting as the administrator of your Page. However, if you want to make a personal contribution, you may choose to switch your "persona" and post or comment as yourself.

With your Facebook Page, your intention should be to get more Likes (followers) and engage with them; think of "likes before leads". Getting more Likes for your Page means more eyeballs and activity on your posts each day. So put out content that people will want to see.

> A good way to get deeper engagement on Facebook is to post updates on things that are not directly related to purchasing one of your products.

Facebook is an excellent traffic source for many small businesses. As your Facebook Page gets more Likes, you'll start to notice increased traffic to your website.

What can you post?

There's a whole array of different types of content you can post. So it's not difficult to mix things up and keep it interesting. Here are some ideas:

- Links to your pre-existing blog posts or web pages.
- Links to interesting material elsewhere on the web.
- News from your reception.
- Press mention about your practice.

Clinics in the Cloud

- Relevant videos (your own or otherwise).
- Practice milestones.
- Industry news, trends and changes.
- Link to a tweet from a fan.
- Relevant humour and cartoons
- Photos of practice, events or staff.
- Uplifting stories.
- Tips and health advice
- Events and invites.
- Inspirational quotes or images.
- Polls, post a survey or ask a question.
- Problems you solve for your patients.
- Links to downloads (stretching cheat sheets etc.)

These are all the things that people will want to see. Some of these won't have anything to do with your practice. Remember that this is a social and relaxed environment, where you can build stronger relationship between your brand and your followers in the long run.

Remember who your audience is and what their expectations are. Facebook provides various tools for you to measure engagement.

Keep posts short, useful, interesting. Add longer, detailed content to your blog and post a link to it in your Facebook Page. It's a good way to keep traffic flowing between your mediums.

Posts that include a photo or video generate between 100-200% more engagement than text-only posts. Try to find a self explanatory and interesting image to go with your post. Don't just use meaningless stock photos.

Focus on the lifestyle around your service; you make people healthier, more independent and capable. This is a great message to leverage as a theme for your posts.

Getting Likes

If you are new to Facebook, a "Like" is a form of currency. When users find something useful or interesting – i.e. something they like – they can let the author know it by clicking on the "Like" button. This is a form of engagement between the author and follower, which also ripples through to other connected users. For example, friends of my follower may get notification that my follower liked my post – which may draw their attention to my original post.

It's a simple yet effective way of interaction and discovering new things.

Letting followers post to your Facebook Page

By default, your Page will allow your followers to post to your Page's Timeline. Such posts would appear in with your own (i.e. posts by the Page administrator). This is generally a good thing, and it encourages interactivity and engagement.

However, it's a double-edged sword. You may want to configure your Page settings to block certain keywords or enable the profanity filter if you find certain people abuse this feature. You can also turn off posting by anyone except the Page admins, or enable moderation of posts before they are visible. With moderation enabled, the Page admin would need to approve each post before they are allowed on your Page Timeline.

In the spirit of engagement and community-building, you should respond to people when they post something on your wall, or make a comment on your posts – even if it's nothing more than clicking the "Like" link. Let them know that you have seen their contribution and appreciate it.

Remember that your Facebook Page is a public place. There will be negative posts and comments – as in any business. How you handle these and respond to them will make all the difference on your Page, just like in your business. Don't just simply delete negative posts and comments without a thought.

If a follower consistently posts inappropriate material or hassles other users, you can ban them from your Page.

Private messages

As the Page owner, you can't initiate private messages with your followers (i.e. people who Liked your Page). However, as the page administrator, you may receive a private message in your Inbox from a follower – to which you can respond. This is great for personal communication with your followers. Keep your eyes peeled for private messages; it won't look good if someone contacted you and you missed or ignored it.

Events, Offers, Contests and Groups

Facebook Events are a great way to notify your followers of a calendar event, such as an open day at your practice. Your followers can respond to your event by letting you know if they're "attending", "not attending" or "may be attending". If someone will be attending, then their friends will be notified in their News Feed – thereby helping you reach more people. As the date of the event approaches, it will remind the attendees.

For a successful event, you should use a good headline and write up an enticing description. You can also remind your followers of your event periodically by posting additional invites via your Facebook Page.

Facebook Offers works essentially like a coupon. You post a discount to be redeemed via your Facebook Page. Users claim the offer. Facebook prompts users to share their bargain grab with friends. The activity appears on friends' news feeds.

With your offer, you can specify an expiration date, choose your audience and a budget. It's important to note that Facebook Offers work more like Facebook Ads in that you can target your audience according to specific demographics and location. Hence this is a paid feature. How many people you will reach with your offer is determined by your budget (among other things). Consider your attention-grabbing headline, description and other details before posting your offer. You can't edit it after it's posted (although you can cancel it).

When someone claims your offer they'll receive an email with details about how to redeem it at your practice. Try a limited size offer first – test how well they work for you without blowing a big budget. Ensure that your offer is simple and genuinely good from the recipient's point of view. Don't burden them with unnecessary terms and conditions. Your expiration date must be realistic, yet create a sense of urgency for an impulse purchase.

Besides Facebook Offers (i.e. feature offered by Facebook), you can also conduct your own offers and contests. You can simply post a message on your Facebook Page consisting of an offer such as "Call our reception today and make an appointment to receive a voucher for a free half hour massage". As long as you have a good number of active followers on your Facebook Page, you can make do without the paid version of Facebook Offers. Such offers are also a good way to encourage more people to like your Page and become followers.

Contests can be fun and engaging. Using your imagination, you can come up with contests such as "Give this photo a caption" – where the most "liked" comment will receive a prize. Such contests are very effective, since you can generate plenty of activity quickly as people scramble to ask their friends to like their comment – all the while you are receiving more eyeballs from not only your followers but also their friends.

Just remember not to give away your core service. Offer something supplementary such as a short massage, dental check-up or GaitScan. Doing regular campaigns will tell you what your audience is interested in and what works for you. Besides growing your follower base and interacting with them, you could be driving additional business through your doors.

Later you can even experiment with using offers and contests to build your email subscriber list – by requiring your audience to sign up to your newsletter (outside of Facebook) to be eligible for the offer. With some imagination and testing, you can generate yourself a nice little pipeline to drive people to become followers, to leads, to prospects and then into paying clients.

Facebook Groups are closed spaces for private discussion and sharing to connect with specific sets of people such as your staff. Groups offer privacy options to limit who can find, join, participate and view activities.

Think of Groups as private Pages where you can discuss internal news about your practice. It may be something to consider, especially if you have multiple locations and lots of staff.

Check ins

If you're a regular Facebook user, you'll be familiar with the concept of "checking in". When you check in somewhere, you're letting your friends know where you are. For example, you can check in at the Colosseum in Rome and attach a selfie for your friends to see. Similarly, you can check in at your favourite local Indian restaurant. Check ins are added to your timeline and viewable on your friends' News Feeds.

Obviously, checking in really makes sense for mobile users as the process involves selecting from places nearby (based on geo-location of your mobile device) by default. If someone wants to find a practice in a particular city, places their friends have recommended, rated or checked in to will be displayed higher.

As a local business, having people check in at your practice is a good way of social marketing. You can even encourage people to check in by offering something in return. However, first thing to check is – are you check in ready? Strengthening your Page's connections and making sure your basic information is up to date will help people find your business.

First of all, you need your Facebook Page set up under category of "Local Business". You can drill into more specific subcategories (business types) too. Then, you need to ensure that your address and other contact details are correctly entered.

It's possible for Facebook users to "create" a place to check in – this usually happens if a place is popular but doesn't have a Facebook Page configured as a Local Business. So it may be that there are existing check in places created for you. If you find this, you can claim and merge these into your Facebook Page.

Facebook Wi-Fi

Facebook Wi-Fi at your business allows Internet access to the visitors to your practice in return for liking your Page and checking in. All you need is a router that supports this feature and some configuration. As a result, you can drive social activity for your Facebook Page and be more discoverable locally and online – with minimal setup and fuss.

This is still quite new, so Google for "Facebook Wi-Fi" to research if this is something you could offer.

Google+

Note that "Google" and "Google+" are different things. Google offers users many services, such as search, Gmail, YouTube and Google Docs. Google+ is a "social layer" across these products and services.

Google+ can be used just like more popular social media platform, Facebook – both personally and in your business. In fact, Google+ has established itself as the second largest social media site in the world with more than 1 billion accounts and 500 million monthly active users.

There are many similarities and parallels between Google+ and Facebook. In your personal use, you can make connections with other people and organise them into "Circles", which are groups of related contacts such as friends, colleagues, referrers, clients etc. You can share an update publicly or with the people in your circles in the form of text, photos, links, videos, or events. You can create Google+ Pages for your business (like you can create Facebook Pages) and use it to reach your clients and prospects.

> Google isn't just a search engine. It's a company that offers search as one of its many services. Other services include YouTube, Google Docs, Gmail and Google+.

You need a Google account to access the pieces of the Google+ puzzle. Getting a Google account is free – in fact, if you use Gmail, then you already have a Google account with which you can login and use Google+. Go to **plus.google.com** to sign up or login to Google+.

Setting up your new Google+ account is easy, with prompts along the way. We won't go into any details here, but remember to fill out your profile with as much detail as you want. If you have a YouTube channel, you can link it up with your Google+ profile.

Once you're logged in and using Google+, you'll see your "Stream", a feed of posts and updates from your Circles. This is the same thing as Facebook's News Feed. As well as sharing your posts with certain Circles, you can also filter your Stream to only show updates from selected Circles. Similarities with Facebook continue; instead of "Liking" something in Facebook, in Google+, you would "+1" it. You can share and comment on posts. Your profile and settings are pretty much parallel to what you're offered by Facebook.

One standout difference in using Google+ is that unlike Facebook, you can "follow" anyone simply by searching for and adding them to one of your circles. There is no "friend" concept. Unless they add you to a circle in return, that person will not see any of your updates and you will only have this person's public posts displayed in your Stream.

Google+ for business

Google+ allows you to create a presence for your practice, like Facebook. So there are many similarities between Facebook and Google+ for personal and business use. However, you'll probably find that many of your friends and followers on Facebook aren't active on Google+.

So what's the benefit of setting up and maintaining separate personal and business profiles in Google+? The answer is "because Google+ is a part of Google, and Google means a lot to your business". Google+ is considered not only a social destination, but also a professional/business network. Due to its integrations with the Google ecosystem, a strong Google+ presence for business brings significant advantages for content creators, authorship and boost in search engine listings for your business to put you ahead of your competition. It connects you with more clients in more ways, assists in improving your website SEO, increases your credibility and even helps to drive your Google AdWords budget further.

There are various services and features offered by Google+ for business. These can get confusing, especially since some are changing and being called different things lately. Here's a quick summary to get you going.

Google+ Pages

Google+ Pages is essentially a Facebook Page equivalent. A Google+ user can create a Google+ Page for just about anything (hobby, band, club, local business etc). You can post updates on your Google+ Page the same way as you would post to your own personal profile.

The key difference from Facebook Pages is that Google+ Pages are more integrated with Google searches. That means a Google+ Page has a better chance of being listed in search results for a related keyword.

Google+ Local

Formerly known as Google Places, Google+ Local is a business listing directory – similar to Yelp or Yellow Pages. Chances are your practice is already on this directory, showcasing your business name, location and contact details. It also enables a pin do be dropped on Google Maps for your location when someone searches for your business. Your listing would have been automatically created by Google, using your details taken from public sources.

This default "unclaimed" listing does not allow connections with other businesses or services, reviews or social engagement. It's pretty much a bare-bones, basic listing.

If your business already has such a default Google+ Local listing, you should claim and verify it by going through a simple verification process. Verification involves having Google call with a PIN number (or send it to your physical address via regular post). When you supply this PIN number to your Google+ account, Google verifies that number (or address) is correctly supplied.

This verification process converts your listing into a Google+ Local Business Page and lets you make changes to your listing as required, via your Google+ account.

> You can search for your listing by visiting
> **plus.google.com/local**

Note that whether you claim your default business listing in Google+ Local or not, the public are able to leave "reviews" about you. We'll get to reviews later. Chances are that Google is already serving up your business listing when someone searches for it in Maps, Google+ and even the regular Google search results. Having a Google+ Local listing that is claimed and managed by you allows you to control exactly what information Google provides.

If a default Google+ Local listing hasn't been created for your business, you can't simply add your listing. Instead, you would need to create a Google+ Local Business Page which would then list your business within Google+ Local.

Google+ Local Business Page

A Google+ Local Business Page is simply a Google+ Page created (by a Google+ user, i.e. you) for a business, and categorised as a "Local Business". Pages created for local businesses offer different features and functions than other types of Google+ Pages. A Google+ Local Business Page combines the business listings aspects of Google+ Local and the social and communication features of Google+ Pages. However, it's common to refer to these simply as Google+ Pages.

When you choose the "Local Business" category, the information you provide on your Google+ Page can also appear in Google search results and on Google Maps.

A Google+ Local Business Page is ultimately what you want to setup and use for your business presence within the Google+ framework.

Multiple locations

If you have multiple practices, your first thought may be to create separate Google accounts for each. However, this isn't a good idea, and it may even cause trouble.

The correct approach would be to use the same Google account to create separate Google+ Pages for each location, so they could all be found or discovered independently via Google's search and mapping tools.

SEO and other benefits of Google+

Google indexes pretty much everything online. Hence it knows that your business website, blog, Google+ Page, YouTube channel and various other online listings are all connected – as online presence of the same business. Having consistent name, address and phone details goes a long way for this, as well as ensuring that your profiles are fully and accurately filled out everywhere online.

Supplying correct and consistent address information for your business's Google+ Page will enable it to be found easily in Google Maps, with a pin or a label highlighting your location.

Although Google+ doesn't have the same traction or user-base as Facebook, its integration and framework means your overall online presence can greatly benefit by taking Google+ seriously.

It's worth noting that when a general public user is logged into their Google account, their searches, preferences and online activity are all tracked by Google. This helps Google to personalise search results and make them even more relevant to each user. That means that two users (one logged into their Google account while searching in Google and the other is not logged in) could get different search results.

Thus, the followers of your Google+ Page will see more personalised search results where your website, blog posts and videos will be ranked higher for relevant search keywords.

Besides this, Google+ makes it easy for your followers to rate and talk about your business within their circles. As they participate and interact with your presence via +1s and comments, your profile will be raised higher.

Businesses get the biggest benefit out of Google+ when they start connecting to other businesses and prominent local individuals. Besides people that directly follow your Google+ Page, your overall listings can get a boost in search engine results pages if you have an active Google+ Page with many comments and +1 activity. Google deems this activity as an indicator of popularity and assumes that there will be more people out there that may be interested in what you're saying.

This is a big deal, since traditionally, website ranking was based primarily by indicators such as how many other prominent websites linked back. Nowadays, social activity on a business's social media profiles contribute greatly as an indicator to a website's ranking and also other integrated presence alternatives such as blogs and YouTube videos.

Google Authorship

Google Authorship connects your Google+ profile with other places online that you contribute content, such as your blog. When set up correctly, your Google+ profile details (photo, name, contact details etc.) can display in Google search results, along with blog posts and other content you have authored online.

Google Authorship essentially means you are recognised as a supplier of articles and information. How far this recognition reaches depends on the amount and quality of material you publish online.

This is great for extending your credibility and authority in your field. It's also fantastic for increased click-throughs from search results to your website or other content you've created.

> Note that Google Authorship will be linked with your Google+ (personal) Profile; not your Google+ Page.

To set up Google Authorship, start here: **plus.google.com/authorship**

Your Google+ Page

The first thing to do is to check if there is a default Google+ Local listing for your business. As discussed, Google may have already created a default listing for your business using data from public sources.

If you find a default listing, you'll need to claim it before you can edit it. Otherwise, you can create your own Google+ Page.

Your Google+ Profile

Whereas Google+ Pages refer to business presence, Google+ Profiles refer to personal presence. By getting started in Google+, you will be given your own personal profile.

Before you delve into Google+ Pages and claiming Google+ Local listings, you should spend a moment to fill out your own personal Google+ Profile. Adding information about yourself, a profile photo and cover image and finding friends already using Google+ is very similar to how things work in Facebook.

You can start following other thought leaders, news providers, people you like and general friends simply by adding them to Circles. From there, your Stream will start populating with posts, just like your Facebook News Feed.

Google offers plenty of assistance and video courses on using Google+ both personally and for business. Once you have your bearings right, you are ready to explore, claim and create your Google+ business presence.

Searching for and claiming your Google+ Local listing

Note: the process of creating a new Google+ Page for your business actually involves a "search for existing listing" step. However, you can still search for an existing page if you are interested in what it looks like before you claim it.

Go to **plus.google.com/local** and search for your business by name and location. Note that your listing may appear under your practice name, company name (if different) or even a personal name. It's possible for professionals to have their default

Google+ Local listing under their personal name, such as "John Smith, Podiatrist".

If you find your listing in search results, click to view the full page. It may already have some public reviews or even photos uploaded from other users, so don't be surprised. Find the section on the page that says something like "Is this your business?" and click the "Manage this page" button. This will require account verification as mentioned earlier. Follow the instructions provided by Google for verification.

You can go ahead and complete your profile and update any incorrect information even without completing the verification steps. However, your edits won't show up on Google unless you complete the verification steps. By selecting "Local business" as your category, you will in effect convert your listing into a Google+ Local Business Page.

Later in this section, we'll go through some important settings for your Google+ Page.

Creating a Google+ Page

Once you're logged into your Google+ account and viewing your profile, you can select "Pages" from the main navigation drop-down menu at the top left.

You will see any existing pages that you own or manage. There will also be a button labelled "Create a page". You can also go directly to this link: **plus.google.com/pages/create**

You'll need to choose "Local Business or Place" as your category. This is important.

Next, you'll be able to search for your business to check if it already exists. If not found, you'll need to confirm that you've entered the name and location details correctly, and that you wish to continue adding your business details.

Ensure that all contact details are entered correctly and choose your business type/category, such as physiotherapist, chiropractor, dentist etc. Unless you visit your clients at their homes or some location other than your business venue, leave the "I deliver goods and services to my clients at their location" checkbox alone.

Confirm your details and continue. Your business will be added and your Google+ Page created.

You will then need to go through the verification process as before. For a new listing, you may be only presented with the postal verification option.

Managing your Google+ Page

You, as the business owner, will want to own your Google+ Page, even though you may not always want to manage or post to it daily. Google+ Pages offer two types of administrators:

1. Owners
2. Managers

Each Page can have one owner; this is the user who creates or verifies a Google+ Page. This ownership can be transferred if required. The Owner can then nominate up to 50 managers. Of course, they would need to have Google accounts and be Google+ users.

Assigning other users as managers is a good idea, to help spread the workload and keep your Google+ Page fresh. Only the owner can add/remove managers or delete the Page.

Who are you logged in as?

Let's clarify one common point of confusion: once you start viewing and managing one of your Google+ Pages, your logged in "persona" will be of that page. This means that even when you visit your Google+ Home / Stream, you will be proceeding as not your personal profile, but your Page.

This is useful because you'll probably want to have different Circles, Events and Hangouts depending on whether you are using Google+ as you (personally) or your business (page).

> You can switch between personas easily enough, by clicking on your user icon at the top right of Google+ at any time.

Linking to your website

Linking your Google+ Page and your website is important for a number of reasons. It helps to connect with your clients and prospects online for a start. It also provides information to Google that can be used to help determine the relevancy of your website to searches in the Google search engine.

This can be done by adding a small unique code on your website. When Google sees this code, it will verify the connection of your Google+ Page and your website.

To get your unique code, go to your Google+ Page profile (accessed via the main navigation drop-down menu at the top left). Under the "About" tab, click the "Link website" button next to your website URL and follow the steps.

Grab the code provided and paste into your website's <head> tag. Your website developer or support guys can help with this. Once the code is added to your website, you can use the "Test" button at your Google+ Page to verify and complete the linkage.

Furnishing your Google+ Page

You may proceed to fill out and furnish your new Google+ Page, even if you have not yet completed verification. Now is a good time to:

- Assign any managers
- Add an introduction about your business
- Upload photos
- Add your business hours information
- Ensure your contact details and website are up to date

You can then view your Page Profile (different from your personal profile) via the main navigation drop-down menu at the top left. From there, you can change your cover image and start posting messages/photos/videos. You should also click on the default logo next to your cover image and upload your own logo or image.

From the main menu, you can view your Page's settings to set your preferences for notifications, subscriptions and more.

Posting to your Google+ Page

Posting to your Google+ Page is the same in many ways as posting to your Facebook Page. You can post news, updates, offers, specials, photos, FAQs, videos and more. You can also target your audience per post, whether public or directed at Circles or private posts for specific individuals. Posting guidelines are the same as per Facebook.

A few other niceties with Google+ are that you can add formatted text to your posts and photos, use #hashtags and view the flow-on sharing activity of your posts via "ripples". These will start making sense to you, as you get comfortable using Google+.

Just like in Facebook, you can allow your followers to post to your Google+ Page. As with Facebook, you can restrict or moderate posts as required in case you need to.

Notifications, comments and messages

As with Facebook, there are many ways to communicate in Google+. You'll receive notifications whenever someone comments on or shares one of your posts or sends you a message directly. It's very important to keep an eye on your notifications so that you don't miss any opportunity to connect with people.

> Notifications are available at the top right of Google+, marked with a "bell" icon.

Managing your Circles

Circles are a means of segmenting your audience. You can create Circles such as clients, members, referrers, local businesses and staff. Thus you can send relevant messages to your followers.

> Managing your Circles can become time consuming; you may want to designate a manager to do this for you.

Remember that the people in your Circles will not receive your posts or updates in their Streams, unless they too have added you in one of their own Circles.

Promoting your Google+ Page

Filling out your Google+ Page profile in full, and linking to your website (covered earlier) is the first thing to do in promoting your Google+ Page. Then, assuming that you have an active personal profile in Google+, you can let your personal friends and followers know about your new Google+ Page, and ask them to follow it. Also ask anyone nominated as your Page managers to do the same with their own friends.

Besides your friends and family, follower numbers will only increase as you post relevant and interesting content to your Google+ Page. Finding, following and interacting with other local businesses, thought leaders and news sources will also build momentum over time. Using appropriate #hashtags will help people search for your posts.

Hosting online Events or a Hangout On Air (like an online seminar) focussed on specific topics of interest can also help you get a lot of exposure to your Google+ Page.

Placing website plug-ins like the +1 button and Google+ Badge on your website will help drive traffic to your Google+ Page too. Your web developer or consultant can help with these.

As with Facebook Ads, you can use Google's AdWords or Google AdWords Express for paid promotion of your Google+ Page. But try the other ideas first.

Ripples

Ripples tell you how interested people are in your posts by giving you a visual representation of who has shared your posts with whom. This is also good for getting a feel for the most active and influential followers so you can target them separately or thank them as appropriate.

Ripples can be viewed via the popup menu for each post – click on the post's menu button at its top right.

Communities, Hangouts & Events

Similar to Facebook Groups, Communities in Google+ facilitate discussions with other users around specific topics. It's Google's version of a group or discussion forum. You can search for and join a community or go ahead and create one yourself. Communities may be public or private. Posting to a Community is much like sharing to one of your Circles.

Hangouts are one of the most popular features in Google+. With a Hangout, you can host a live group chat like a text-based chat room. Furthermore, you can have up to 10 participants in an interactive and private video chat. This is great for live Q&A sessions with your clients or prospects, or video conference calls with your staff online. You could also host a Hangout On Air, which is like a webinar that you present to a large group of viewers. It's excellent for building authority in your field.

Events in Google+ work just like they do in Facebook. You can schedule and promote any event you like, such as getting people to join in on your live Q&A Hangout. Great for driving new business.

Check ins

Check ins in Google+ work the same way as per Facebook. You can search for a nearby location (e.g. a Google+ Local business) and let your friends know that you were there.

Reviews

Reviews in Google+ Local Business Pages give you a way to see what your clients think of your business. Consumers have more faith in what other consumers say than what you say. If you've researched anything online with an intent to purchase, you undoubtedly paid attention to other people's reviews – whether you personally know these people or not. Reviews benefit both businesses and their clients. Businesses can improve their offering based on what clients say and consumers can make informed decisions based on other people's experiences.

Consumers can leave reviews and a star rating (out of 5) for businesses on Google+. Remember that even Google+ Local listings that have not been claimed can receive reviews and rating. As a business owner with a properly set up Google+ Page for your business, you can review and respond to reviews.

These public reviews are hard to fake, since they aren't anonymous as each review is attached to a Google+ user. So in many ways, reviews are better than testimonials for a business. Testimonials often need to be "requested" from clients, so they sound generic, boring and not credible. Whereas reviews are often left by clients of their own free will because they genuinely enjoyed your service (or not). Google+ reviews aren't directly controlled by the business and what is publicly said about you is largely out of your control. This makes them more trustworthy for consumers.

Having lots of great reviews for your business is an excellent way to make potential clients feel at ease enough to come in and see you. You can find the reviews left for your business under the "Reviews" tab of your Google+ Page's profile.

Although you can't actively moderate or pick and choose reviews left for your business, you do have the opportunity to flag inappropriate reviews. A negative or rant review about your business doesn't qualify as an inappropriate review. However, anything that's unlawful, discriminatory, advertising or spam, off-topic or conflict of interest (e.g. by a disgruntled former employee) can be contested.

If you only have a Google+ Local page and it has not been claimed, then you can still receive reviews; however you will not be able to respond to them.

Getting reviews on Google

To encourage reviews, you can actively remind your clients to leave a public review of your business on your Google+ Page. It's easy to look up a business and leave a review.

By having an active presence on Google+ and responding to posts and reviews, your clients will notice that you value their input and respond with more reviews.

You can also leave lots of (genuine) reviews for local businesses in your area. This can encourage a return of favour.

Two very important notes on getting reviews:

1. You cannot solicit reviews from people through incentives.
2. Consider limitations that may be imposed by your governing bodies or associations. Reviews may fall under restricted activities along with use of testimonials in the marketing of certain services, especially related to health.

YouTube

We've already covered some interesting facts and statistics about video and YouTube in an earlier chapter. We've also illustrated that you don't need big budgets for professional agencies, and that you can pretty much take full advantage of YouTube for your business using equipment you already have.

Remember that YouTube, like many other things, is just a tool. Use it to supplement your website and online presence along with other tools for maximum and lasting benefit.

It's important at this stage to remember that Google owns YouTube. Hence your Google account which you used in the last section to login and use Google+ will also let you do some amazing things on YouTube.

We've already covered videos and video production in an earlier chapter. So here, we're looking specifically at YouTube and leveraging it for your business.

YouTube for business

Your business's presence and activity on YouTube will translate very well into additional exposure and increased search engine listings – the same way your Google+ Page did for your business.

Also note that with Google's current push for Google+ we can expect more streamlined and social activity between Google's tools. This is especially important when considering your online interaction with your audience. This also means that most of the services covered here will be continually evolving and by the time you pick up this book, things may very well be different. So as with everything else in this book, remember to use the information here as a start in your journey to broadly understand the different pieces and how they fit together.

Your YouTube Channel

Currently, YouTube is evolving from a video-based site to a channels-based site. Just like you can have a Facebook Page or a Google+ Page for your business, you can also have a YouTube Channel where your followers are known as "subscribers" of your channel. There are now some excellent features in channels to not only adjust the look and feel to suit your brand, but also link up with your other online content and presence. It's an exciting medium to turn viewers into loyal fans.

Just like you have a personal Facebook or Google+ profile, your Google account gives you your own YouTube account where you can upload videos of your kids, cat or anything else you like. However, for business use, you'll want to create a separate channel to upload and showcase your videos.

Again, it's about content and authority

Remembering that your videos on your YouTube Channel are just another form of content, you'll want to produce videos that people will find useful and interesting.

YouTube has many social media features built in – you can upload content and visitors can like (+1) and share your content as well as leave comments. It's a good medium to converse with people who like what you offer. So the overall goal in using YouTube for your business is once again to increase followers and spread your message.

It's also worth noting that since YouTube is owned by Google and it's the second most popular search engine in the world, getting good exposure and achieving loads of interest means that you'll be rewarded with benefits such as improved search results for your website and other online presence. All that equates to more business for you.

We've already covered the types of videos to shoot and editing your videos earlier in this book, so we won't cover any video production related topics here.

Logging into your account

You don't need to be logged into YouTube to search and view videos. However, to upload videos and manage your YouTube Channel, you need to be logged in. We discussed how your personal Google account can grant you access to just about every Google service, such as Google+.

Remember that when you create a Google+ Page (as described before), you are given separate "personas" or accounts – so that you can use various Google services "as yourself" (personally) or "as your business".

If you went through the process of creating your Google+ Page for your business, you will now also have a YouTube Channel for your business. Because they're all connected, logging into your personal Google account will give you easy access to your other accounts / personas – i.e. your YouTube Channel for business – simply by clicking on your account icon at the top right and choosing the linked account.

Whenever you're uploading or managing videos for your business, make sure that you're logged in as your business. You don't want to accidentally upload to your personal account and share a video publicly, only to have viewers become interested in seeing what else you have in your channel (i.e. your personal videos).

If you still don't have a Google account (even after reading the last section on Google+), visit **plus.google.com** to get one.

Setting up your Channel

As with setting up your Facebook Page and Google+ Page, there are several things you should do when setting up your YouTube Channel. As always, the specific mechanics involved may (will) change over time. Here are some of the basics you should pay attention to.

You may be eligible for a custom URL, to help visitors identify you such as youtube.com/channel/yourbusinessname. Once you are signed in as your business account, go to your advanced account settings at **youtube.com/account_advanced** and click "Create custom URL" under Channel Settings. Note that once you set a custom URL, you can't change it.

> Upload your channel icon and channel art. Think of these as your profile picture and cover image for your Facebook Page and Google+ Page.

If you have a good "overview" video already, you can use it as your "trailer" – i.e. video that starts to play when someone visits your channel. Normally, videos that auto-play on a website are a big no-no, but within the YouTube context, it's more acceptable because it's expected. The trailer video will only play for non-subscribers and won't annoy regular visitors of your channel. So be sure to include a call-to-action for subscribing to your channel.

Under your Channel's "About" tab, add a Channel description and links. The links should include your email address, website and links to your other social presence including your Facebook Page, Google+ Page etc. In your description section, be sure to include your contact details, address and a link to a Google Map page for your location. Search engines can detect such linkages and raise the overall profile across the board. By connecting with your social media accounts, you can have YouTube post links to your newly uploaded videos to your Facebook and Google+ Pages automatically.

> Avoid advertising and monetisation features unless that is to be your business model. Don't distract viewers. Ads are annoying.

Once you have enough videos, you can start grouping them into playlists and sections on your channel home page. These help viewers find and watch related videos focussed on specific topics or types of content (i.e. Q&A videos or intro videos for new clients). It makes sense to place more compelling videos at the top of your channel and playlists.

Managing your YouTube Channel

The managers you assign for your business's Google+ Page are also (conveniently) the managers of your YouTube Channel. They can upload and manage your videos and respond to comments from viewers.

Uploading videos to your channel

Once you have your video file exported from your editing software, you'll need to upload it to your YouTube channel.

To start your upload, ensure you are logged in as your business account. Click on the "Upload" button at the top of the page and follow the instructions. Depending on the file size and your Internet connection speed, the upload can take from a few minutes to an hour or more. A progress bar will indicate how much longer you'll need to wait. You must leave the upload page open in your browser during this time.

Once uploaded, YouTube will process your video and prepare it for your channel. You can enter your title, description, keywords, tags and other settings during this time.

Use a good thumbnail – it could make the difference between being seen or ignored. You can choose from one of the 3 auto-generated thumbnails YouTube provides you. To use your own thumbnail image, you will need a verified account. You can verify your account at **youtube.com/verify**. Verification also allows you to upload videos longer than the standard 15 minute limit.

Generally speaking, you'll want to set your videos as "public" so that everyone can view them. If you produce videos for specific people or clients and don't want these videos to be viewed by anyone else, you'll need to flag them as "unlisted" or "private". Unlisted videos can still be accessed by the public, however they will never show up in search results (the only way to view them is if you give someone the direct URL). Private videos can only be viewed by the people you nominate, regardless of whether they know the URL or not.

Now you may want to add your new video to an exiting playlist – or create a new playlist.

YouTube tools

YouTube offers a variety of tools to make your videos more interactive and valuable (both for your viewers and you as the channel owner).

YouTube's video editor allows you to perform basic editing of your videos online. This feature is not as flexible or useful as desktop video editing software (covered earlier in this book), but can suffice for simple jobs or for use in emergencies (when you don't have access to your desktop software).

Music can be added as a background soundtrack for your video from within YouTube. Lots of royalty free music is available, and you can search by genre, mood, instrument or duration. When you find music you like, you can use it in your video via YouTube's video editor or download for use with your desktop video editing software.

Annotations are text overlays and clickable hotspots that you can place over your videos to enrich the video experience with additional information, interactivity, and engagement. You can specify when and where these clickable regions appear and link through to relevant websites or resources online. For example, you can mention, "Subscribe to our newsletter" and provide a link to the web page with your subscription form.

> You can add "subscribe" links to your videos in your channel by using the "InVideo Programming" features.

Video SEO

In early days, YouTube was the place for one-hit, user-generated viral videos. However, now that it's a major business marketing tool, you need to think about your approach to videos and long-term channel strategy.

Just like your website content, blog posts and social media activity, content on YouTube can contribute heavily towards your business's online profile and ranking in search results.

It's not uncommon to see web pages with video embedded in them (or the video itself in YouTube) get exceptional rankings. Videos can also get indexed by Google faster than web pages. According to many sources, it's 50 times easier to end up on the front page of search results using video. Why? Because people love video and Google aims to deliver what people want. Here are some tips to help you get most SEO out of your videos:

Offer value

Make good videos that people will want, value and share. Google gives more visibility to more popular videos and videos that people watch in their entirety.

Optimise for search

Google can't view and index what it sees in your video (like it can with your website content). Hence it relies mostly on the information you provide about your video, such as title, description and keywords. From there it can still deduce how popular your video is and how it links with other content online. These are combined to enable Google in determining how to rank your videos in search results.

Optimise for attention

Ensure every video you upload has an attention-grabbing title that contains good keywords. Add relevant and useful tags to help viewers find your video based on its content. Use good descriptions that give the viewer an indication of what the video is about and include any links you may make references to in your video. Remembering that only the first few lines of your video description are shown initially (rest can be viewed by clicking "show more"), it's worth including your website link as the first line.

Video SEO is still quite new – especially in the field of local practice marketing. So jump on the video bandwagon today to get ahead of the competition.

Getting mileage from your videos

Remember: going viral is not the aim for your videos. Slowly and steadily building a good content base is the best way to build and keep getting regular traffic over time.

We've already discussed bookends, annotations and playlists. Make sure that you use these tools effectively.

Once you've uploaded your video, you can embed it to your website or blog post and share in social media sites. Besides the title, description and other meta data you attach to your video, the context provided by your website pages will help the search engines figure out what your videos are about.

When you share your videos on your social media sites, encourage your followers to share with their friends. Remember that more and varied exposure and shares of your video will show Google how popular it is.

Promoting a video in an email or eNewsletter is a great idea. Even though you can't embed videos into an email, you an include an image of your video featuring the familiar triangular play button. Link this image to your YouTube video. Images like this get more clicks than just a text links.

Link-up related videos with annotations. You can place clickable hotspots to link-up videos in a series such as "view next video in this series". This is a good way to get more videos viewed at a time.

You can send a message to all your subscribers by posting on your channel home page. This is good way to notify them when you have a new video. Include a link to your video or playlist in your message. These messages appear in your subscribers' news feed.

You can cross-promote with other channels. This is similar to guest-blogging which we covered earlier in this book. Find YouTube channels that have an overlap in your target viewers, yet aren't direct competitors. Get in touch with the channel owner and create useful videos for each other's channels. Remember to place links to your channel and website into these videos and their descriptions.

As with other social media, keep an eye out for comments and messages and respond to them. Engage personally with your viewers and encourage interaction to build your community and a loyal following. People have viewed your content and have something to say – it's important to pay attention to them.

Video analytics

YouTube Analytics allow you to track how many people are viewing your videos and what they're interested in. You can get insights into your most active days (or time of day), where your visitors found your video, where they are located in the world and other demographic information. You can see when there's a spike in viewership and work out what caused it. It's also valuable to see how far you keep viewer attention and at what point viewers leave your video. Combined with comments left by viewers, you can gather up lots of intelligence to plan future videos and improve your content offering.

If you use Google Analytics for your website, you can connect it with your YouTube Channel to tap into richer data about your channel's performance and audience behaviour. However, the setup can be a little tricky and you'll need to be familiar with the use and interpretation of Google Analytics.

Other social channels

LinkedIn

Not so much a social media site, but more a professional networking tool, LinkedIn is frequented by 20% of Internet users who are primarily white collar professionals.

You may have good luck finding other professionals to connect and network with (both to receive referrals or staff to employ). However, it's unlikely that LinkedIn will be a good source of leads itself. You can also use it effectively to build your professional authority by updating your status or posting links for your blog posts and videos.

Remember to fill out your profile in full and join some key networks or groups.

As people start finding you on LinkedIn, you'll start getting requests to connect. Whether you connect with someone or not is your choice; some people get quite strict about the people they connect with. My preference is that if someone is a friend of a friend or in my industry, I will readily connect.

Twitter

Around 16% of Internet users are on Twitter, which is basically a micro-blogging platform. Instead of writing well thought out posts, Twitter caters more to the on-the-fly blurting of ideas and shares. Each post is limited to 140 characters. Twitter attracts a young and educated audience who have ideas and links to share.

Twitter can be a great source of news if you follow the right people in your industry. However, Twitter is not fundamentally "local", like Facebook or Google+. It's also harder to get your message heard and interact meaningfully with your followers or groups.

There's also somewhat of a learning curve for correct use of #hashtags, @mentions, retweets etc.

> Unless you have all the time in the world, you're probably better off focussing on Facebook, Google+ and YouTube than pushing Twitter.

You can use Twitter to search for certain keywords to find potential clients. For example, you can conduct a search at **search.twitter.com** for "back pain" to see who has mentioned these words in a recent tweet. This seems like a good way to proactively reach out to someone and offer him or her your services or direct them to a video with a reply tweet. However, as before, there is currently limited opportunity to narrow down search results by local region. So this is not likely to produce worthwhile new business for a private practice.

Pinterest

With reach of about 12% of Internet users, Pinterest is a highly visual photo and idea collection website. It attracts primarily younger women. If this is your target demographic, you should consider Pinterest.

Pinterest is basically place for people to collect, categorise and post images of things they like. These are often pictures they stumble across while surfing.

Pinterest is good for businesses that offer products or services that could be represented visually, such as crafts, beauty and health accessories etc.

There is some opportunity for private practice to use Pinterest, depending on what you offer. For example, you can tell visual stories and cover events such as boot camps, activities, funny staff moments and other fun and interesting photos. These could also be used on your Facebook and Google+ Pages.

Instagram

With reach of about 12% of Internet users, this mobile-based photo sharing site generally attracts the under-30 crowd.

The stereotypical photos taken on smartphones and shared on Instagram include the infamous "selfie", food about to be consumed, pets, friends, travel and social activities. Unlike Pinterest, the photos uploaded are not categorised around specific themes.

For private practice, same photos that are used on Pinterest could be used on Instagram. Again – if you have the time and resources, you could maintain Pinterest and Instagram accounts in addition to Facebook and Google+. Hey, you're taking photos anyway – why not reach more people for a little additional effort? Just make sure that you can keep up with comments and engagement from followers.

Foursquare

Foursquare is essentially a "check in" service, currently with a user base of about 50 million. It was a great idea when it came out in 2009, however it has become quite redundant once Facebook and Google+ (with their massive user base) added this functionality to posts.

One advantage of Foursquare is that a business can list special deals and promotions for its users to claim when they are in the local area.

It won't hurt to claim your business listing with Foursquare, however, if you have limited time and resources, you'll want to focus on Facebook and Google for this aspect.

"Getting" social media

Social media takes time to show visible impact on your business. It's one of those things that will click one day and have you wondering how you ever ran your business without it. However, it can seem a bit of a struggle until that tipping point. It'll be especially confusing if you haven't ventured into the world of social media even on a personal level.

Email marketing is more familiar than social media. So you may feel more comfortable with it. So let's take a look at some parallels:

With email marketing, you have email addresses of people who have opted in (asked to receive emails from you). You send out regular emails with valuable content and some offers. They open your emails and click on links or offers contained therein. They may even forward your email to friends.

With social media, you have a bunch of followers who want to receive posts from you. You post regular messages/updates with interesting news and links. They read your posts and click on links or offers. They share your posts within their social network.

So the things to keep in mind are largely common sense (once you get going) and similar to email marketing (and even other forms of marketing).

1. **Choose a platform.** Focus your resources on one social media platform initially, be it Facebook, Google+ or YouTube. Choose one that that fits your needs and master that first.

2. **Generate regular content.** This can be blog posts, articles or eBooks. Use your social networks to drive prospects back to your website by linking to this content.

3. **Commit.** You'll need to set aside regular resources to create content, engage with followers and review activities. Set aside resources and schedule time. Treat your social media like a micro blog. This will build trust with your audience.

4. **Engage your audience.** Ask questions, share interesting photos and facts – have fun.

5. **Be authentic.** Show your true self and open up your doors. Let your followers see who you are and what you stand for. Share what you're genuinely excited about.

6. **Focus on relationships.** Listen to conversations, respond to questions and offer advice. Check back regularly. It's easier to build one-on-one relationships via social media than other marketing channels.

7. **Follow others.** Following others is a good way keep a tab on what's going on with them. Search for users you want to connect with specifically. Seek out relationships.

8. **Post relevant and useful things.** You can share useful advice and tips directly on your social media channels. It's OK to share other interesting (or simply fun) posts, as long as they're relevant.

9. **Experiment and learn.** Try different kinds of posts and check the pulse from your audience to see what they respond to. Use the analytics and insights tools available for each platform. When you hit upon a post that has exceptional response, promote it further – reach other people who will want to join the discussion.

10. **Leverage for positioning.** Use social media to position your practice as a leader and authority in your area.

11. **Leverage for brand loyalty.** Keep your brand in the forefront of people's minds.

12. **Reward with specials and offers.** Offer tangible value which followers can claim at your practice. Provide clear calls-to-action to generate leads and new clients. At minimum, thank your followers.

13. **Drive conversation.** Ask for opinions. Open up a friendly debate. Show you're listening. Respond to comments and acknowledge participation. Treat all client feedback with respect.

14. **Drive offline events.** Your online participation helps drive offline events, such as open days and special programs.

15. **Ask for followers.** It's OK to ask people to "subscribe" to, "follow" or "like" your page or channel. If they don't, check the above tips.

16. **Have fun.** People on social media are mostly there to escape their daily grind.

Remember, Facebook, Google+, YouTube and other social networks are simply tools. How YOU use them is what counts.

Building social momentum

Remember: it's a marathon, not a sprint. This has often been the pain point for most local practices when it comes to marketing via social media. But once you have the momentum, social media has proven countless times to be an excellent source of new business.

So, you've opted to start with a Facebook or Google+ Page (or both), created and furnished your profile, linked up your website and blog and completed whatever else the platform offers in getting started. What now?

Remember that useful and interesting content is at the root of growing your social media following. However, simply having lots of followers is useless without relevance and meaningful interaction. Otherwise you may as well run a "funny joke of the day" page, with 20,000 followers and no new clients through your doors.

Get into your posting rhythm before you start asking people to follow your page.

Your posting rhythm

We've already discussed the many types of content you can publish and your publishing rhythm.

Most posts in social media are likely to be short and quick. Even when you want to share your most recent blog post that took an hour to write, you wouldn't copy and paste it into a Facebook or Google+ post. The better way to do it would be to simply provide an attention grabbing message plus a link to your blog post. Doing it this way ensures that you keep driving traffic to your website (mother ship) and away from the distractions of social media. There, you could tease them with other useful content, encourage them to sign up to your newsletter, download other material or make an appointment to see you.

Of course, you won't always have articles, blog posts or eBooks to share. Most often, you'll be sharing simpler, quicker posts for variety.

In the early days of your social media presence, make sure you have a few dozen good and interesting posts – preferably over a period of a week instead of a single day. Link to your most valuable published content from your website, blog or YouTube Channel. Include a special promotion in lots of fun posts. This is so that when potential followers reach your page, there will be some good reason for them to stay and explore. If you grab their attention, they'll want your future posts in their News feed or Stream.

From here, you simply need to maintain your content rhythm. Remember – publishing regular content on your website or blog and posting regularly to your page(s) is one of the key elements of a successful social media presence.

With Facebook and Google+, aim to post a few times a day. Vary the time of day you post to maximise your reach. Your followers will be logging in at different times of the day. There are tools available to schedule social media posts, so you don't need to drop everything to post something every day.

Getting your first followers

It's now time to tell your family, friends, clients and everyone else in your address book about your new Facebook or Google+ Page and invite them to follow it. You can email them or message them via social media. Make sure you include a link to your new page. Tell them that it's brand new and you're trying to build some traction. Ask them to tell their social media friends about it too.

Then get your staff to do the same. From there, your page will rely on the type and quality of content and posts you share to grow organically.

You can always go back to the basics: putting links from your website to your social media pages is an easy way to get people there. You could also put up signs at your reception or a line on your business card and email signature, telling people to find you on Facebook or Google+.

Demonstrating commitment to the medium by showing up daily, sharing your knowledge and being useful will build trust with your audience.

> Remember: Your fans are not really "yours" – they are merely a "rent-a-crowd", held by their interest in what you say, do or offer.

Shares, likes, +1s, thumb ups & comments

Getting responses to your posts and engaging with your followers will amplify your voice and keep your posts and shares more relevant. Your posts will display more prominently in followers' feeds and it'll be easier to find your page.

People use social media differently. Instead of watching TV, I use Facebook, Twitter and Google+ mostly to get my news from specific pages or people I follow. For many others, social media is a chill out destination, away from their daily grind.

We know that good content is appreciated. However, as we also know that things like headlines, titles and visual presentation can make a massive difference to capturing your audience's attention, generating interest and curiosity. Based on audience response, you'll soon be able to strike a balance between delivering information, educating, entertaining and promoting your practice via your posts.

Here are some post formats that have been proven to get more Shares, likes, +1s, thumb ups and comments.

- **Craft your headlines.** Well-written headlines and posts can really put your followers in the mood to view your link, like your post or provide comments.
- **Use interesting photos with your posts.** Posts with photos have been proven to have a higher interaction, as they draw more attention. Choose photos carefully – the photo alone in many cases can generate curiosity.
- **Ask questions.** i.e. "Do you remember your first sports competition?" or "what is it you like most or least about visiting a dentist?" You can ask an interesting question that begs an answer to draw responses from your followers. People will supply comments to your post in response.
- **A or B.** E.g. "Would you rather jog or swim?" Such questions are easy to read, understand and will readily get

answers and interaction. It can help polarise audiences, which is good to drive discussion. This is also a good way to run a simple poll or survey.

- **Fill in the blank.** Posting a question with a _____, and asking to fill in the blank is another classic response generator.

- **Inspirational images.** The Internet is awash with images of inspiring quotes. When you find one that is relevant to your business, post it. It's a good way to get likes and comments.

- **Local news.** What's going on in your town? Have you gotten involved with a local event? Did you catch up with some clients? Photos (with permission) would be great.

- **Seasonal posts.** Is it that time of year? Are the finals on?

- **Case studies.** With permission and as appropriate, you can showcase success stories from your clients. Just check that your governing bodies or associations allow this sort of thing.

- **Myth busters.** Busting common yet interesting myths is a great way to get interest and demonstrating your knowledge.

- **Go backstage.** Letting your social media followers in on certain secrets or the way you do things behind the scenes can help them feel like a part of something more than just your business.

Engaging with your followers

Your goal is to get people's attention with your posts. So when you receive a comment, you must not ignore it. They have given you their valuable attention and even the time to respond to your post.

Depending on the nature of the comment, you may need to comment back, answer a question or give tips etc. This is the start of a public conversation. Other people may well join in.

At the very least, you should "Like" their comments, as an acknowledgement and appreciation for their comment.

> Regular and useful content will get attention. Focus on relationships and engagement will help build your business. Understanding the platform and your audience will help with both.

With your posts and follow up comments, you need to encourage interaction and discussions as much as possible. Remember the "throwing a party" analogy? Some people will readily engage, whereas others will be shy. As a good host, you should try to involve everyone. You can mention people directly in your posts (they will receive specific notification about this). It's a good way to draw people in. Inspire and hold conversation. This also involves knowing when to listen!

> Why are you on social media, if you don't even respond to posts?

Social media platforms offer numerous ways to alert you when people interact with your posts. Learn these and watch them carefully.

Having a consistent voice and opinion and demonstrating your knowledge and care for your followers will help build your status as an authority.

Finding the sweet spot between information and marketing can take some time. Occasionally asking your followers to take some action will be well perceived once you have earned trust with them. You'll soon be able to simply ask for likes and +1s.

Privacy and security

Do you have privacy and security policies in your practice? Your social media channels need to adhere to these policies, since they're an extension of your business. Keep in mind what you post, share or say – especially if it involves someone.

Citations, reviews and reputation

A citation is when your business name, address, and phone number (NAP) are listed on the web. You could have citations from Google+ Local, Yelp, Yellow Pages and various directories. Citations from authoritative places help boost your visibility in Google Maps and local search results, by allowing Google to verify that all the different listings are in fact the same business and also to build a profile of your business's online reputation.

NAP: Name, address and phone

We covered creating (or claiming) your Facebook and Google+ business pages. Since your business name, address and phone number are your main data points to connect your various citations, you need to ensure that these are consistent (i.e. identical), with the same spelling.

Some directories create business listings automatically to grow their database. It's a good idea to keep a document on your computer of your NAP, which you can refer back to, so you can check that any such listing is accurate. If not, you should look into claiming and updating that listing.

Directories and review sites

Google+ is the most important listing you need to get right. Facebook is a close second. But there are many other places to get citations.

Yellow Pages, Yahoo Local, Bing Local and Yelp are other obvious ones. They too have integrated their listings with their own mapping and search features. However, they remain relatively low-key since they don't have Google's weight and momentum. They also lack the social media layer and various integrations that Google+ offers.

In any case, you should (must) check whether your business is listed with them and verify your details. If you don't have a listing, make sure you add it to broaden your reach and online presence.

Spending a little time with Google, searching for any directories specific to your niche is a good idea. If you're not on the list, see if you can add yourself. Note that this doesn't mean you should get sucked into every directory that offers paid listings. Unless you can see clear and independent benefits to paying for a listing, don't bother just for citation value. The major directories all offer free listings (including Yellow Pages).

Your local chamber of commerce will probably offer a good citation for you. You may also find some local networking groups, local events websites, local charities and local press opportunities to get your NAP listed.

Reputation management

Consumers increasingly rely on online reviews for making informed purchasing decisions. So what's your online reputation? Have your clients given you online reviews? Are they all glowing with 5 stars?

When a single negative review can really affect your business, how do you protect yourself? Especially when the major reputable review sites remain independent and won't let you moderate the reviews you receive? This is where reputation management comes into play.

Consistently getting negative reviews should be an indicator to you that something in your business is amiss. However, that's a topic for a different book.

Firstly, you need to be on the ball. Whether you like it or not, people can leave reviews for you. As long as these reviews are fair and objective, this is a great thing. Most review sites offer opportunity for businesses to respond to reviews from clients. Some even have safeguards in place to prevent or remove irrelevant, fake, spam or rampant reviews. However, here we'll focus on the client who was genuinely not happy with your services.

When you receive the odd negative review, use it as an opportunity to publicly make good. It's a great chance to remedy the situation and it'll go a long way for the person who felt wronged. Handling such issues with flair, transparency, professionalism and compassion (genuine interest in people) can turn things around for you despite the initial gripe. This is just common business sense, and the online platform can help you push your positive message just as quickly as how fast the negative review could travel if left unchecked. Ignoring negative feedback is the worst thing you could do.

> Always respond to any review less than 4 stars. Simply say "thank you" for the 5 stars.

One other way to reduce the impact of bad reviews is to get plenty of great reviews. Offering great service and then letting your clients know that they can leave you a review is usually quite ok. However, check with your governing bodies or associations about this, since some will frown upon such things.

Crossing your channels

You can see by now how so many different strategies work hand-in-hand to help your online presence flourish and grow your business. This extends to offline marketing also. You don't need to start ignoring traditional methods.

Traditional marketing (outbound marketing) is still surprisingly useful in many areas. For local businesses, things like flyer drops in letterboxes of local residences can still be very effective. However, you'll find that significant time and investment is required with these. Since nowadays people are generally tuned out to the traditional marketing efforts, you may need to run your tests for extended periods of time.

Regardless, you should try to integrate any traditional marketing with your website. For example, you can have a landing page on your website with a special offer which can be claimed when the visitor subscribes to your newsletter. You can use a QR code on your Yellow Pages advert. You can have an offline promotion and collect email addresses at your reception for newsletter subscriptions. You can send out postal letters or invites followed by email messages two days later to extend your reach and response rates. Print out your newsletters or information sheets from your website and post them to your clients. Businesses are excellent results from cross channel marketing ideas like this.

Get creative, try new ideas. See what works for you. Even Google and Facebook do this in their own marketing! You may have received a voucher for free AdWords advertising in the post – Google? In the post? Yes! It works.

If you have an idea but don't know how to implement it, chat with your web developer.

Testing and measuring

Knowing what to measure and how to read results is a crucial skill in business. You can try a dozen things, but if you can't take away lessons from your activities, you're just wasting time and money.

We've covered a lot in this book, and hopefully I've inspired you to go out and try a few new things. You can see that there's a lot you can be doing, so you'll need to pick and choose your activities based on your needs, resources and of course, what you're comfortable with.

> "Half the money I spend on advertising is wasted; the trouble is I don't know which half."
> ~ John Wanamaker

By testing and measuring, you'll be in a better position to work out what works. It's obviously an iterative process and can take a long time to pin down the correct indicators and then use them to base your marketing decisions.

You're at an advantage – with the tools, services and support available to you, there has never been a better time to do all this as easily, cheaply and quickly as you can today. Then it's a simple matter of picking what works and repeating it.

Key indicators

Being able to attribute outcomes to specific actions is an important skill. This is how you decide what's working and what isn't. Unlike the days of traditional marketing, there are many tools to test and measure the effectiveness of your online strategy.

Being able to determine which types of content or posts generate most interest will help you understand your audience and plan future topics. Being able to tell which marketing offers resulted in the most appointments or sales will help you target your message with greater accuracy. Being able to measure the amount of money spent per new client acquisition will tell you whether your promotion was profitable or not.

Every business is unique; setting arbitrary key performance indicators (KPIs) from the outset isn't a good idea. What is a good idea is to understand the importance of testing and measurement, learn from your activities and tweak as you go along. Remember: be dynamic, not static!

Decide on your ultimate outcomes. In most cases this will simply be "more appointments". From there, you can start to think about the data you need to measure and how you can obtain it. This may be as simple as viewing the number of enquiries received at your website. However, remember that many people will be picking up the phone to make an appointment after viewing your online presence too. You will need to consistently ask new clients how they found you and record it so you can attribute sales to your activities correctly.

Tools of the trade

Here are some of the most common tools you can use in testing and measuring your online strategy activities and effectiveness. A whole book can be written about each of these tools, so this will only serve as an introduction.

Google Analytics

Google Analytics is a free yet powerful tool. By inserting a snippet of code into your website (your web developer can help with that), you'll be able to start measuring a plethora of statistics and indicators.

In the olden days, metrics such as "hits" on a website were popular, since there were no better alternatives to measure. Analytics can tell you about your visitors, where they came from and what they were interested in at your website. It can tell you how much time they spent and whether they "converted". It integrates seamlessly with Google AdWords – the advertising platform – so you can measure whether your advertising dollar is returning you a profit.

Google Analytics is a very comprehensive and powerful tool – so it's common to feel lost in it when you first jump in. It's also constantly evolving. However, there are loads of videos and YouTube channels dedicated to helping small businesses understand and use Google Analytics effectively.

> A common trap is "paralysis by analysis." It can take quite a while to get a grasp on what the stats all mean and using them to your advantage.

Initially, focus on these three metrics:

- **Visitors**: How many people are coming to my website? Where are they coming from?
- **Leads**: How many visitors converted to leads? What did they convert on?

- **Sales**: How many leads converted to sales?
- **Bounce rate**: This measures how many people come to your website but leave after viewing the first page they see. It indicates that they arrived at the wrong website, or didn't find what they were looking for straight away.

This will be a good start – as you get more comfortable, you'll start to discover the power tools and indicators to help you fine-tune your website, marketing and online strategy. So don't fall into the trap of relying on these metrics as key indicators of your online strategy effectiveness. It's easy to get more traffic via an AdWords campaign or writing lots of new blog posts. This doesn't always mean more sales. But Analytics can clue you in on what does and doesn't work, if you know what to look for.

Google Webmaster Tools

Google Webmaster Tools allows web masters and marketers to check indexing status and optimise visibility of their websites. Generally speaking, it's a tool for advanced users, website managers and developers who understand SEO and various other technologies. It should be used in tandem with Google Analytics for best results.

You can access Google Webmaster Tools via your Google account.

Social media measurement

The three most important social media platforms, as far as your business is concerned, all have built in analytics tools. These are:

- Facebook Insights

- Google+ Pages Insights
- YouTube Analytics

Since these are still under heavy development and their features are changing (improving) constantly, we won't be covering them in this book. There are many online resources and YouTube videos about them – simply search for it.

It goes without saying that you need to familiarise yourself with these tools and dashboards to help you determine what your audience is interested in and plan future content. Remember your goals with social media – is it just to get more "likes", or more business resulting from better knowing and interacting with your prospects?

Measuring promotions

Landing pages

We covered landing pages earlier. These are often stand-alone pages at your website, with the intent of receiving visitors in response to a specific campaign (e.g. link from a newsletter promotion). They are great for testing marketing ideas and measuring client interest.

You could try variables such as "long-copy sales page" vs. "short copy". You could experiment with including video or different graphics on your landing page. There are many resources online about these.

Landing pages could also be used to determine the effectiveness of campaigns – simply by measuring how many visitors clicked on a link in your AdWords campaign, call-to-action, post, email or newsletter and arrived at your landing page as a result. This could help you prepare more compelling promotions.

So before launching a landing page, ensure that you're tracking it for not only how many visitors are arriving from your promotion, but also whether it's converting those visitors into sales or other ultimate outcomes.

> Set up a system to measure the metrics of your website so you can reproduce successful campaigns and scrap failing ones.

Landing pages can be used to measure offline campaigns too. For example, you can create a QR code with a link to a landing page, so you can measure how many people used that QR code to find you.

It's important that your landing pages should not be indexed by search engines. Your target audience should only reach that page via a link you provide in an email or direct message. Being able to find your landing page via a search engine will skew your numbers.

A-B testing

A-B testing is an advanced strategy that involves 2 versions of the same landing page (i.e. A and B). These versions generally differ by a small factor, such as:

- Headline

- Call-to-action
- Colours used
- Images used

By sending half of your prospects to one version and the other half to the other version, you'll be able to judge which the more effective landing page (or offer) was.

Use this same concept with Google AdWords and Facebook Ads, to see which one converts better.

The key to A-B testing is to ensure that you only use incremental and small changes between the two variations – otherwise you won't be able to attribute any significant outcomes to a specific change. For example if you changed the headline, the call to action and the background images on A and B versions of a landing page, and your results indicated that A performed 500% better than B, how will you know what really caused this?

Remember – you can take your learning from one A-B test and then apply it to your next test, where you'll change something else. The idea is to determine the best combinations over a range of tests.

One other important factor is that A-B tests require large numbers. Having a few people participate won't give you a statistical significance. Hence this strategy is only useful once you have lots of followers, subscribers or visitors to your website.

Personalised URLs

Examples of a personalised URL would be:

- www.mywebsite.com/offer/**JaneSmith**

- www.mywebsite.com/**DrDaveRadson**

You can see a name embedded in there – and if that was your name, you would be curious to check it out, wouldn't you?

Personalised URLs can be used very effectively to reach specific people, with specific offers. They're also easy to track and measure, simply by viewing your Analytics.

Imagine being able to easily tell whether your local doctors have viewed their specific offer pages at your website, when and how many times. You can also then track their other activity at your website, such as what other pages they looked at. This could be valuable insight when targeting referrers for your practice. It can also help you make warm calls later, knowing that you offer has been viewed a few times by your intended recipient.

Remember to use a clear name in the URL. Opt for full name, rather than a generic first name. And don't forget to remove the page after it has served its purpose.

Making sense of data

Remember that it takes lots of practice, experience, effort and patience to be able to look at a bunch of analytics and determine what's really going on. Don't get hung up simply on vanity metrics like number of likes or visitors. There is so much more you can learn about your visitors, website and social media.

Do one thing at a time so you can measure without "contamination".

Metrics are pivotal for pinpointing the exact pain points of your website, email communication and social media presence. By doing small but constant adjustments and measuring outcomes, you'll be able to maximise your tools for generating visitors, leads and ultimately, sales.

Ethics and legal

You are a trusted member of your community and this puts the weight of certain responsibility on your shoulders. Besides simply ethics, there may also be governing bodies in your field who dictate a certain level of conduct.

You're perfectly healthy...
I don't know what to prescribe

When marketing your health practice, you need to bring ethics and the law into the equation. At the end of the day, you're an expert and people will trust and rely on you to do the right thing.

Noting the large grey areas when it comes to some health services, it's ultimately up to you as the professional to judge what's right and wrong.

Your ethics (and law) will decide such things as whether a treatment is needed and what qualifies as over-treating someone. This is obvious stuff you covered in your first year of school.

However, note that there may be less obvious regulation around the business aspect of your practice. Things to consider include whether offers for free or discounted care and use of testimonials on your website are appropriate. You could even be barred from using unsolicited, public reviews in social media, depending on your governing bodies.

Regulations vary by country and even by state. Always use an appropriate disclaimer and be careful what you advocate in your posts and publications online.

If in doubt, you must do your research or seek professional advice to avoid getting into trouble.

Use of copyrighted material

With so much material available today, infringing on copyright is rather easy to do. Is your content original or did you "borrow" parts from another source? Do you have the rights to use those photos on your website?

It's not nice to receive a surprise email one day telling you that you've been caught out using someone else's work without proper rights, attribution or permissions. In the best case, you may be asked to remove the material in question. At the other end of the scale, you may be up for a hefty fine.

Remember that according to copyright laws, claiming ignorance (e.g. "I didn't know that photo required licensing") will not save you.

To avoid issues like this simply make sure that you're the author of your work, or have the rights to claim it as your own. If you must include someone else's material, get permission and then reference it properly.

With images, make sure that you either take your own photos or purchase the correct license from stock image libraries. There are many such libraries where you can buy stock photos for a few bucks. It's not worth the risk.

About the author

Yalcin started out as a software and web developer in 1996, before Google was Google. Working on start-up clients and small business strategies, he solved business problems in the online space before moving onto contract jobs for various government organisations.

Yalcin later worked on digital campaigns for multinational marketing agencies such as Publicis and BBDO. Some of the recognisable brands he worked on include Nike, Hewlett Packard, Coca Cola, National Australia Bank, Seek, Fosters, Nestlé, Village Roadshow Entertainment, L'Oréal, Sensis, Mercedes, Dulux and Cadbury.

When he became a father, he left the frantic agency life and returned to his original passion, small business. In 2007, he crossed paths with several chiropractors and physiotherapists. This is when he noticed that irrespective of where they are located or what stage their business is at, that same key questions and problems keep coming up for businesses in private practice – especially online.

He founded his own start-up in late 2008, now known as PracticePulse. Having created the 3 Ps of online strategy for private practice (presence, publish, profile) he now brings the experience, best practice and digital solutions to health businesses in private practice around the globe.

Yalcin has a Bachelor of Engineering (Software) degree and a pending Masters in Entrepreneurship and Innovation. He is a father, martial artist and a wannabe photographer.

Contact: yalcin@practicepulse.com

About PracticePulse

PracticePulse is a website development and support company. We work exclusively with health care and wellness practitioners in private practice that do amazing things for their patients but fail at promoting themselves online and running their clinics efficiently.

We've heard the same questions over and over from thousands of businesses around the globe. We understand the nature of private practice.

Leveraging our extensive research, knowledge and expertise, we provide our clients with a well planned website as the perfect springboard on which to build an online strategy (presence, publish, profile). Our state of the art, custom-built platform makes it child's play for them to not only try new ideas, but also measure results and decide what works — for them. This may be blogs, social media, newsletters, being found in search engines or a mix of all this, or whatever the future holds.

Friendly technology is only the start. Fanatical proactive support, useful advice, regular updates and constant monitoring leaves our clients feeling empowered. Ultimately, they can deliberately and sustainably increase the number of new and repeat clients they see each month and do what they do best.

We believe it's time for health care businesses to stand up and gain the recognition and prosperity they deserve. Our mission is to see our clients reach their business potential, just like they love to see their own clients reach their health potential.

Our aim is for PracticePulse to be the preferred provider of website services for private practice worldwide, known for the online success we bring to our clients.

Website: practicepulse.com

Thank you.
Now kick ass online.

Yalcin Yilmaz.

"

www.ingramcontent.com/pod-product-compliance
Lightning Source LLC
Chambersburg PA
CBHW060331220326
41598CB00023B/2668